Your Greater Is Coming

Discover the Path to Your Bigger, Better, and Brighter Future

Joel Osteen

Nashville   New York

ALSO BY JOEL OSTEEN

A Fresh New Day Journal

All Things Are Working for
Your Good
*Daily Readings from All Things Are
Working for Your Good*

Blessed in the Darkness
Blessed in the Darkness Journal
Blessed in the Darkness Study Guide

Break Out!
Break Out! Journal
Daily Readings from Break Out!

Empty Out the Negative

Every Day a Friday
Every Day a Friday Journal
*Daily Readings from Every
Day a Friday*

Fresh Start
Fresh Start Study Guide

I Declare
I Declare Personal Application Guide

Next Level Thinking
Next Level Thinking Journal
Next Level Thinking Study Guide
Daily Readings from Next Level Thinking

Peaceful on Purpose
Peaceful on Purpose Study Guide
Peace for the Season

Rule Your Day

Stay in the Game

The Abundance Mind-set

The Power of Favor
The Power of Favor Study Guide

The Power of I Am
The Power of I Am Journal
The Power of I Am Study Guide
*Daily Readings from The
Power of I Am*

Think Better, Live Better
Think Better, Live Better Journal
Think Better, Live Better Study Guide
*Daily Readings from Think Better,
Live Better*

Two Words That Will Change
Your Life Today

With Victoria Osteen
Our Best Life Together
Wake Up to Hope Devotional

You Are Stronger than
You Think
*You Are Stronger than You
Think Study Guide*

You Can, You Will
You Can, You Will Journal
*Daily Readings from You
Can, You Will*

Your Best Life Now
Your Best Life Begins Each Morning
Your Best Life Now for Moms
Your Best Life Now Journal
Your Best Life Now Study Guide
*Daily Readings from Your
Best Life Now*
*Scriptures and Meditations for
Your Best Life Now*
Starting Your Best Life Now

Your Greater Is Coming
Your Greater Is Coming Study Guide

Your Greater Is Coming

FaithWords
Hachette Book Group
1290 Avenue of the Americas, New York, NY 10104
faithwords.com
twitter.com/faithwords

First Edition: October 2022

FaithWords is a division of Hachette Book Group, Inc. The FaithWords name and logo are trademarks of Hachette Book Group, Inc.

The publisher is not responsible for websites (or their content) that are not owned by the publisher.

The Hachette Speakers Bureau provides a wide range of authors for speaking events. To find out more, go to www.hachettespeakersbureau.com or call (866) 376-6591.

Library of Congress Cataloging-in-Publication Data
Names: Osteen, Joel, author.
Title: Your greater is coming : discover the path to your bigger, better, and brighter future / Joel Osteen.
Description: First edition. | Nashville : FaithWords, 2022.
Identifiers: LCCN 2022019469 | ISBN 9781455534418 (hardcover) | ISBN 9781546002840 | ISBN 9781546003533 | ISBN 9781455534425 (ebook)
Subjects: LCSH: Expectation (Psychology)—Religious aspects—Christianity. | Waiting (Philosophy) | Encouragement—Religious aspects—Christianity.
Classification: LCC BV4647.E93 O88 2022 | DDC 248—dc23/eng/20220606
LC record available at https://lccn.loc.gov/202201946

ISBN: 9781455534418 (hardcover), 9781455534425 (ebook), 9781546003533 (large print), 9781546004561 (special edition), 9781546004554 (special edition)

Printed in the United States of America

LSC-H

Printing 1, 2022

CONTENTS

CHAPTER ONE

Your Greater Is Coming

We all face setbacks in life, things we don't understand. We may have lost a loved one, had a friend walk out of our relationship, or are dealing with an illness. When we go through loss and bad breaks, it's easy to think that's the way it's always going to be. But our God is a God of restoration. He doesn't stop every difficulty, and He doesn't keep us from every challenge. But He promises He will pay us back for the wrongs. He will restore what's been stolen. David says in Psalm 71, "You have allowed me to suffer much hardship, but You will restore me to even greater honor." The suffering is a setup. God allows the difficulty, not to make you miserable but to restore you to greater honor. He never brings you out the same. He makes the enemy pay for bringing the trouble.

When you're in tough times, you need to remind yourself that it's not how your story ends. The loneliness, the bad break, or the anxiety is not your destiny. Greater is coming—greater joy, greater strength, greater relationships. The setback in your finances, the contract you lost, or the unfair childhood didn't stop your purpose. Greater opportunities are coming, greater favor is coming, greater influence is coming. The enemy brought the difficulty to set you back, but he didn't realize it's setting you up for God to

> *The enemy brought the difficulty to set you back, but he didn't realize it's setting you up for God to show out in your life.*

show out in your life. He may have meant it for your harm, but God is turning it to your advantage.

When you're in difficulties, when life doesn't seem fair, you'll be tempted to get discouraged and lose your passion. Keep this phrase down in your spirit: *Your greater is coming.* God didn't bring you this far to leave you. He wouldn't allow the pain if it were going to keep you from your destiny. It's just the opposite; it's going to thrust you into your destiny. The apostle Paul says, "These light afflictions are for a moment, but they are working in you an eternal weight of glory." The trouble is temporary, but the glory is permanent. The key is to not stay focused on the suffering; stay focused on the glory that's coming. It may be tough now. Life has dealt you an unfair hand, but that suffering is not in vain; it's serving a purpose. It's leading you to greater favor, greater anointing, greater victories.

I love David's attitude. He says, "God, You have allowed me to suffer much hardship," but he doesn't stop there. He could have stayed focused on all of his bad breaks and said, "God, I don't understand it. Why didn't my father believe in me? Why did he leave me out in the shepherds' fields when Samuel came to anoint the next king? Why is King Saul trying to kill me? I haven't done anything wrong. Why are all these people slandering me, trying to ruin my reputation?" Instead, he says, "God, I've had a lot of bad breaks. I've suffered much, but I know this: You will restore me to greater honor." He was thanking God for greater in the middle of the difficulty. When

> *When you're in tough times, you can either talk about how big the problem is or talk about how big your God is.*

you're in tough times, you can either talk about how big the problem is or talk about how big your God is. You can be complaining about the trouble or you can be thanking God that the trouble is only temporary.

If you're going to see the greater, you have to do as David did. In the middle of the suffering, start declaring that greater is coming. If the medical report doesn't look good, while you're taking the treatment you have to say, "Father, thank You that greater health is coming. Thank You that the number of my days You will fulfill. Thank You that I will run and not be weary." When you're fighting depression, anxiety, or fear, don't sit around thinking about how you're never going to get better. In the middle of the battle, you have to say, "Lord, thank You that greater joy is coming. Thank You that You're pushing back the forces of darkness." When it seems as though you're stuck in your career and your dream looks impossible, say, "Father, thank You that greater favor is coming. Thank You that You're opening doors that no man can shut, that You're taking me where I can't go on my own." Your attitude in the suffering is what's going to determine whether you come out with greater or whether you get stuck where you are.

Going Through Is the Way to Your Greater

The apostle Peter says, "After you have suffered a little while..." I'm not saying that if you have faith, you'll never have any suffering, never have things that aren't fair, never have situations that aren't turning around. But keep the right perspective. The suffering is not permanent. You may suffer for "a little while"—not for your whole life, not for the next twenty years. Don't believe the

> *Don't believe the lie that what you're going through is never going to change.*

lie that what you're going through is never going to change. Don't believe the lie that you'll always struggle with the addiction, that you'll always have to deal with a sickness, or that you'll always have that trouble at work. The suffering is not going to last. It didn't come to stay; it came to pass. What God started in your life, He's going to finish.

But here's the key: To see the greater, you have to go through the suffering. I wish I could tell you that greater comes by just being positive, just having faith, just honoring God. There are levels you can only reach by going through some difficulties. Don't get stuck in the suffering. Don't get bitter because somebody walked out on you. Don't settle in the depression, thinking that's your lot in life. Don't let the setback in your finances convince you that you'll always struggle. Keep an attitude of faith and go through it. Keep believing when every thought is telling you it's never going to change. Keep talking like it's going to happen when nothing is improving. Keep declaring God's promises when it seems as though it's not doing any good. That suffering is a test. It's an opportunity to show God that you're not going to get discouraged, give up on your dreams, and lose your passion.

Peter goes on to say, "After you have suffered a little while, the God of all grace, who called you to His eternal glory in Christ, will Himself restore you, strengthen you, and establish you." God has already called you to live a victorious life. He's already called you to overcome every obstacle. You've been handpicked by the Creator of the universe. The God who spoke worlds into existence chose you before you could choose Him. The forces trying to stop you are no match for the God who has already called you. Now do as David did and go through the suffering with faith, knowing that your greater is coming. If you keep the right attitude, God Himself is going to restore you. That means that He's not going to send the angels, He's not going to ask Gabriel to do it, but the Most High God is going to suddenly turn

> *When it's your time, you're not going to come out the same; you're going to come out better.*

things around. He's going to suddenly heal, suddenly deliver, suddenly promote. When it's your time, you're not going to come out the same; you're going to come out better.

You may have already passed this test. You've been doing the right thing, suffering with a smile, praising through the pain, worshipping instead of worrying, being good to people who aren't good to you. Get ready. Greater is coming. God is about to do a new thing. Problems that look permanent are about to turn around. Dreams you thought were too far gone are about to suddenly come to pass. The right people, divine connections, are about to show up. Greater influence is coming, greater favor is coming, greater honor is coming. The enemy thinks he is pulling you back to keep you there. He doesn't realize that like a bow and arrow, the more he pulls you back, the farther God is about to shoot you. The enemy thinks he is hindering you, but the truth is that he is helping you. The suffering is a setup. God allowed it so He can launch you to a new level of your destiny. Don't get discouraged by what you're going through. You couldn't become who you were created to be without the disappointments, without the bad breaks, without the struggle. I know it's uncomfortable, and I know you don't like it, but keep reminding yourself that greater is coming.

Everything Is Coming Back

In 1 Samuel 30, when David and his six hundred men were returning from a mission in Philistine territory, in the distance they saw smoke billowing in the sky. It looked as though it was coming from their city of Ziklag. I can imagine that they started walking faster, wondering what was going on. When they arrived home, their worst fears came to pass. The Amalekites had raided their city, burned their houses, taken their wives and children captive as well as all their possessions. Here David was out doing the right thing and the wrong thing happened. It didn't seem fair. But just because you have trouble doesn't mean you're doing something wrong. Sometimes, because you're doing the right thing, you're facing difficulties. There are forces trying to keep you from your destiny. When you understand this principle that every setback is a setup for God to take you further, the suffering is putting you in position for greater honor. Then you won't fall apart when you face bad breaks. You won't get bitter because you have an unexpected challenge. You'll stay in faith, knowing that the enemy wouldn't be trying to stop you if he didn't know something amazing was in your future.

When you understand this principle that every setback is a setup for God to take you further, the suffering is putting you in position for greater honor.

David and his men were so discouraged that they wept until they could not weep anymore. If that wasn't bad enough, David's men were so upset about losing their wives and children that they began to talk about stoning him. David could have sat around depressed, in self-pity, but the Scripture says, "David began to encourage himself in the Lord his God." Maybe that's when he wrote, "I will bless the Lord at all times. His praise will continually be in my mouth." Maybe he wrote, "When I go through the valley of the shadow of death, I will fear no evil, for You are with me." Maybe in those ashes he wrote, "Surely goodness and mercy will follow me all the days of my life." Instead of complaining, he started thanking God that He was still on the throne.

Sometimes you can't find anyone else to encourage you. Your friends are busy, your pastor is out of town, your phone is dead, and you can't find me on television. That's God letting you know that you have to encourage yourself. You have to dig down deep and say, "I am not going to let this bad break, this disappointment, or this injustice steal my joy and sour my life. Lord, thank You that You are bigger than this sickness, greater than this opposition, more powerful than the people who are trying to stop me. I know that Your being for me is more than the world being against me." You have to stir up your faith, stir up your praise. Start speaking victory over your life. Start thanking God that He's fighting your battles, that this too shall pass, that greater is coming.

David prayed and asked if he should go after the enemy. God answered, "Yes, pursue them. You will surely recover everything that was taken from you." You may be in a difficult time when you've lost some things—lost your dream, lost your joy, lost your health. God is saying, "If you get your fire back and start moving forward, you will surely recover everything you lost." The enemy may be laughing now, but you're going to have the last laugh. God has the final say. He saw the injustice. He saw who did you wrong, what didn't work out, what was taken from you. He's saying, "Get ready. Everything is coming back. You're getting back your health, your children, your finances, your dreams, your

> *The enemy may be laughing now, but you're going to have the last laugh.*

joy, your peace." It's not maybe, not there's a good chance, but surely you will recover everything. *Surely* means without a doubt, that you can count on it. God used the word *surely* not for Himself, but for us. He is saying, "Be confident. It's all coming back."

Your Reward Is Coming

David and his men left the city and headed out in pursuit. They were not certain where the Amalekites had gone, but they found an Amalekite slave in a field who had gotten sick three days previous and been left behind to die. David gave him food and water and promised that if he would lead them to the Amalekites, David would spare his life. This young man took them right to the enemy's camp. When you get your passion back and go after what belongs to you, God will have the right people in your path to help you. He'll bring divine connections, people who will use their influence and expertise to take you where you couldn't go on your own.

> *When you get your passion back and go after what belongs to you, God will have the right people in your path to help you.*

When David and his men showed up, the Amalekites were having a big party, celebrating their victory, eating, drinking, dancing. I've learned that sometimes the enemy celebrates too soon. He doesn't realize that you're down but you're not out. You had a setback, but really it's setting you up. The enemy thought the disappointment would cause you to be sour, to give up on your dreams. He thought the bad break would cause you to stay sitting in the ashes, discouraged and bitter. He didn't know you would encourage yourself in the Lord. He didn't know that when you got knocked down, you would get back up again. He didn't know that instead of complaining, you would start praising. He may be celebrating now, but don't worry. Your time is coming. Right now God is arranging things in your favor. He's lining up the right people. He's pushing back forces of darkness. Things are happening that you can't see. If you keep moving forward in faith, you're going to come into promotion, healing, breakthroughs—things that you couldn't make happen on your own.

David and his men attacked the Amalekites and wiped them out. Not a single Amalekite was left in the camp. The Scripture says, "David got everything back that the Amalekites had taken. They rescued their wives and children. Nothing was missing: young or old, boy or girl, plunder or anything else they had taken. David brought everything back." You may have lost some things. Perhaps your loved one didn't make it, and it feels as though a part of you was taken with them, and you have lost the joy you had. Maybe you've struggled with an addiction for so long that you've lost the desire to be free. Perhaps you've accepted that it's too late now and your child is never going to get back on course. God is going to do for you what He did for David. One day you're going to say, "Nothing is missing. I got my joy back. I got my health back. I got my dreams back. I got my freedom back. I got my child back." God is not going to bring you out partially, where you get most of what you lost. God doesn't do things halfway. Nothing is going to be missing.

> *Nothing is going to be missing.*

It was a great victory that David got everything back. But God doesn't bring you out the same. When you go through suffering, your greater is coming. The Scripture says, "David's men rounded up all the Amalekites' flocks and herds and took all their possessions. These belonged to them as their reward." There is a reward

> *You're not just going to come out, you're going to come out better.*

for going through difficulties with a good attitude. We would be grateful if God just brought us back to where we were. But when you go through challenges in faith with your head held high, knowing that God is fighting your battles, then a reward is coming. You're not just going to come out, you're going to come out better.

The Suffering Is a Setup

Back in the 1950s, my father had been pastoring a very successful, growing church for many years. They had just built a beautiful new sanctuary. He was on the state board for his denomination, and his future looked bright. At that time, my sister Lisa was born with something like cerebral palsy. After the doctors told my parents that she would probably never be able to walk or feed her-

> *He realized that there never was a day of miracles, but there is a God of miracles. And He's still alive.*

self, my father went to a downtown hotel for a week by himself to study the Scripture in a new way. He had been taught in seminary that God healed people in biblical times but that period of divine healing had passed away. He read the Scripture that says, "Jesus Christ is the same yesterday, today, and forever." He realized that there never was a day of miracles, but there is a God of miracles. And He's still alive.

My father went back to his church with this new message of faith and victory and healing. He thought everyone would be excited, but it was just the opposite. This message didn't fit their tradition. There was so much opposition that he ended up feeling he had to leave the church. He was very discouraged. He had poured his heart and soul into those people. My mother was twenty-six years old at the time, and she had lifelong friends who never spoke to her again.

Instead of sitting around frustrated and bitter over what didn't work out, my parents went out and started Lakewood. They found an old feedstore that had holes in the floor and cracks in the walls. They cleaned it out, and ninety people showed up for church. My father went from a big prestigious church with a beautiful new auditorium to a run-down little wood building with a fraction of the people. Year after year my father kept being his best, pouring into those ninety people, not listening to the critics. The opposition said that Lakewood would never last, that he was wasting his time. But when you suffer much, God gives you a promise that greater honor is coming—greater favor, greater opportunity, greater influence. Against all odds, my sister Lisa slowly got better and better. Today she's perfectly healthy. And in 1972, Lakewood started to grow, with people coming from all over Houston. It kept growing and growing, and here we are over sixty years later, still going strong.

We all have unfair things happen. People come against us. There are betrayals, and there are sicknesses. It's tempting to get discouraged and say, "God, why did this happen? Why did these people push me out? Why was my daughter born with an illness?" There are some things that we're not going to understand. Don't spend your life trying to answer all the whys of life. That's going to frustrate you. God knows how to work all things for your good. He says that He will pay you back double for the unfair things that have happened. The key is to go through that suffering with a good attitude, knowing that God has promised you that your greater is coming. It may not happen overnight, but God

> *Don't spend your life trying to answer all the whys of life.*

is faithful. He sees you doing the right thing when the wrong thing has happened, taking the high road, overlooking the offense. He sees you being your best at work when people aren't giving you the credit. He sees you standing against the illness, staying in faith when you could be complaining.

Your time is coming. That suffering is a setup. As with my father, you're going to see the hand of God take you where you can't go on your own. Don't worry about the people who have tried to push you down. God is preparing a table for you in the presence of your enemies. They're going to see you promoted, honored, in a position of influence. It doesn't go unnoticed when you fight through health issues with a good attitude, still thanking God, still being good to others. You've gone through the suffering, now get ready for the greater—greater health, greater freedom, greater breakthroughs, greater victories.

Greater Honor Is Coming

In Genesis 29 is the story of two sisters, Rachel and Leah. When a young man named Jacob saw Rachel, he fell head over heels for her. It was love at first sight. The Scripture says, "Rachel was beautiful in every way, with a lovely face and a shapely figure." When God says you're fine, you know you're fine. Rachel had it going on. Jacob asked her father, Laban, if he could marry her. Laban said he could if he worked seven years for him. Jacob worked faithfully for those seven years, but Laban didn't keep his word. He tricked Jacob. At the weddings back then, the brides wore very thick veils, so you couldn't see who was behind the veil. Jacob assumed the bride was Rachel, but it was Leah. The Scripture says, "Leah had weak eyes and was dull looking." I don't know what weak eyes mean, but I know what dull looking is. I have a brother named Paul.

Laban made sure Jacob had too much to drink at the wedding. The next morning when Jacob woke up, he saw weak eyes staring back at him and nearly passed out. He went and found Laban and said, "What in the world are you doing? You know our agreement was for Rachel." Laban responded, "Yes, but our tradition says the oldest daughter must be married first. Work for me another seven years and you can have Rachel." Jacob was so dumb—I mean *so in love*—that he worked another seven years and finally married Rachel, too. But the whole time, Jacob never really loved Leah. All of his attention was focused on Rachel. But Rachel was unable to have children and remained barren. Meanwhile, Leah gave him son after son, hoping this would win his affection, but it didn't change anything. Years later, Rachel finally gave birth to two sons, Joseph and Benjamin.

All those years, Leah lived in a loveless marriage, feeling unwanted, not chosen, marginalized. I'm sure she was tempted to have low self-esteem, to not feel good about who she was. But God sees when you're not being treated right. He sees when you're being overlooked, pushed down, and discounted. Leah could have been depressed and gotten bitter, but she just kept suffering in silence, doing the right thing with a good attitude, not complaining. When it came time for God to choose a family line to bring Jesus through, He didn't choose one of Rachel's sons, even though she was the favorite wife. He didn't choose Joseph, whom we read so much about in the book of Genesis. He didn't choose Benjamin. He chose Leah's son Judah. Jesus came through the tribe of Judah. All of Leah's sons became founders of six of the twelve tribes of Israel.

What's the point? Even when people dishonor you, don't get discouraged. God knows how to honor you. He knows how to cause you to shine. People don't have the final say. They may try to discount you and make you feel less-than. Keep your head high. You're not who people say you are. You are who God says you are.

> *You're not who people say you are. You are who God says you are.*

He calls you a masterpiece. He says you are fearfully and wonderfully made. You have royal blood flowing through your veins. He's crowned you with favor. You may have to suffer in silence at times and do the right thing when it's not fair. You may have to work hard when you're not getting credit and be good to people who aren't good to you. God is keeping the records. When you go through much suffering, He promises that greater honor is coming. Greater favor. Greater influence. Those who discount you now will look up to you one day. People who won't give you the time of day will strive for your attention one day. God knows how to pay you back. He knows how to make your wrongs right.

When you're in tough times, keep this phrase playing in your spirit: *Greater is coming.* The difficulty is not there to defeat you; it's there to promote you. You may have lost some things in the past, and you've accepted that it's never going to happen. This is a new day. Things are shifting in your favor. God is saying to you what He said to David: "You're going to get everything back. Your joy is coming back, your health is coming back, your children, your dreams, opportunities, freedom. I believe and declare that nothing will be missing, large or small.

CHAPTER TWO

It's Just a Matter of Time

There are times in all our lives when we have things we're believing will change. We might be fighting an illness, struggling with an addiction, or dealing with fear, anxiety, or depression. We know that God has promised that He would restore our health, that our children would serve the Lord, that we would be free from the fear. We prayed, we believed, but we don't see anything improving. But what you can't see is that the moment you prayed, the source of what was coming against you was cut off in the unseen realm—the source of the fear, the source of the addiction, the source of the sickness. You may not see any manifestation for some time. There may not be any evidence that anything has changed. This is when many people get discouraged. There will always be a time period when it looks as though God didn't do what He promised. The fear still comes, the medical report hasn't improved, or the addiction is just the same. But what's feeding those things has been cut off. It just looks as though they're still alive. The truth is that the fear is dead, the addiction is dead, the trouble at work is dead. Don't get

> There will always be a time period when it looks as though God didn't do what He promised.

discouraged because you don't see anything happening. It's just a matter of time. What God promised you is on the way.

The Roots Are Dead

One time when Jesus was leaving the village of Bethany, He saw a fig tree off in the distance. He was hungry and walked over to get some of its figs to eat. But the tree didn't have any figs. He said to the tree, "May no person ever eat fruit from you again." He cursed the tree. But after He said it, nothing on the outside of the tree looked any different. It was just as healthy and full as before. I can hear the disciples whisper, "It didn't work this time. What happened? Did He lose His power?" They had seen Jesus speak to a blind man and heal his eyes. They had heard Him speak to the raging sea and calm the wind and the waters. But this time when He spoke, nothing changed. There was no evidence that what He'd said had happened.

But the next morning as they were passing by the tree, the Scripture says, "The disciples saw that it had withered from the roots." When Jesus spoke to the tree, nothing happened on the outside, but inside, down in the roots, the source was cut off. When the roots are dead, the tree is dead. It may still look alive, it may still have green leaves and wide branches, it may look healthy and strong, but it's just a matter of time before the outside catches up with the inside.

> *When Jesus spoke to the tree, nothing happened on the outside, but inside, down in the roots, the source was cut off.*

It may look as though the sickness you're dealing with is still alive, or the anxiety seems as bad as ever, or the addiction is just as strong. You've been praying and believing, wondering why God won't do something. God has done something. The moment you prayed, He cut off the source. That addiction looks alive, but if you could see the roots, you would realize it's dead. It's just a matter of time before the outside catches up. The sickness seems permanent. You feel as though you'll never get well. No, have a new perspective. The roots have been cut off. The sickness is dead. The depression is dead. The poverty is dead. Don't get discouraged because there are still leaves on the tree and nothing looks any different. Psalm 75 says, "The strength of the wicked is being cut off, and the power of the godly is being increased." You need to know that the power of everything that is trying to stop you is being cut off. It may be hindering you now, but it's only temporary. It's not going to last. It's lost its source. Every day it's withering; every day it's getting weaker. On the outside it may look the same, but inside it's drying up.

When Jesus spoke to the fig tree, there was no sign that anything had happened. There was no evidence that anything had changed. Maybe you're believing for something and you don't see any sign of things improving. You're speaking faith over your health, but the medical report is not getting better. You're praying for your child, but he or she is not getting back on course. If you just had some evidence, if you just had a little sign, then you would believe. But this is what faith is all about. You can't be moved by what you don't see; you have to be moved

> *You can't be moved by what you don't see; you have to be moved by what you know.*

by what you know. "Father, thank You that the moment I prayed, You cut off the roots. I know that this sickness is not permanent.

Healing is coming. I know that this addiction is not how my story ends. Freedom is coming. I know that this depression doesn't have the final say. Lord, thank You that it's withering and dying."

Some of the things you're worrying about, God has already done it. You haven't seen it, but in the unseen realm things have changed. The anxiety that you've been praying about, asking God to take away, it's already dead. The trouble at work, God has already cut off the source. Now do your part and stay in faith until it manifests. Keep thanking God, keep talking like you're free, keep thinking like you're healthy, keep acting like you're victorious.

Believe First

I talked to a man who had struggled with an addiction for many years. He said, "Joel, I asked God to help me, but nothing happened." He didn't see anything changing on the outside. It wasn't getting any easier, so he assumed that God wasn't doing anything. He lived with the mind-set that says, "I'm addicted. I can't get free. It's too strong." He was waiting to see the manifestation before he believed that God was working. But faith says you have to believe that when you prayed, God put the miracle in motion. You can't wait for the evidence and then you'll start believing. You have to believe first. You may not see any sign of it, but you have to know that deep down the source of that addiction has been cut off. When you know that the roots have been cursed, you'll have a different mind-set. Instead of thinking, *Maybe it will happen one day*, you'll know it's just a matter of time. God has already spoken. He's already cut off the roots. Now all you have to do is walk it out.

I told that man what I'm telling you: "You may not see anything happening, but the moment you prayed God did something."

Instead of thinking, *One day I'll be free*, try a new approach and say, "Father, thank You that I am free. Thank You that this addiction is dead. Thank You that it doesn't control me, that You've already put an end to it." He started living with the attitude that it was already cut off. He kept thanking God that He was free, talking like he was free.

> *Are you waiting for the evidence to believe what God said about you?*

When I saw him six months later, he said that after twenty-two years of being addicted, he was totally free. Are you waiting for the evidence to believe what God said about you? Are you talking yourself out of it because you don't see any sign? If you get in agreement with God, you'll see what He's done inside show up on the outside. The source of what's trying to stop you has been cut off.

"Well, Joel, it seems as though it's still alive. It's seems as though it's stronger than ever." Don't be fooled by the outside. In our backyard we have some beautiful rose bushes. One day Victoria cut off one of the roses and brought it inside. The moment she cut it off, it was dead. It was separated from its source of life. But what's interesting is that it didn't look dead. It didn't look any different than all the other roses that were still on the bush. It was still beautiful, still colorful, still smelled great. She brought it inside and put it in a vase by the kitchen sink. For a couple of weeks it looked beautiful and healthy. But the whole time it was dead. It was just a matter of time before it withered.

You may have things in your life like that rose. The moment you prayed about the addiction, the depression, or the fear, it died. The sickness has been cut off. But it looks just the same. You don't feel any different. You don't see anything changing. That's okay. That doesn't mean it's still alive. That doesn't mean your prayer didn't work. At some point, like the rose in the vase, it's going

> *The first place we lose the battle is in our thinking.*

to begin to wither. You're going to see what God promised you come to pass. The Scripture says, "Don't faint in your mind." The first place we lose the battle is in our thinking. Thoughts will tell you, *Nothing happened when you prayed. You'll never get well. You'll never break the addiction. You've struggled for years.* Don't believe those lies. The roots have been cut off. It's just a matter of time before you see things change in your favor. What's trying to stop you is temporary.

We have some friends who send us a box of a dozen rose buds every Easter. They have long stems with a rose bud on the top. What's interesting is that even though the rose is dead, even though it's been cut off from the bush, when you put the stem in water, the rose will bloom. It's dead, but it will still blossom. It has no life, but it will still get bigger, expand, increase. There are times when, even though God has cut off something in your life, it will get bigger. Even though He's cut off the sickness, it will increase. Even though He's cut off the trouble, it will blossom. You'll be tempted to think, *There's no way this sickness is dead. It's getting worse. There's no way this anxiety is dead. It's increasing, not decreasing.*

> *There are times when, even though God has cut off something in your life, it will get bigger.*

No, stay encouraged. It may bloom, it may blossom, but it's still dead. It's just a matter of time before it withers. All through the day you have to say, "Father, thank You that the source of this trouble has been cut off. Thank You that You cursed the roots of this fear. You spoke to the addiction. You commanded the sickness to wither and die. So, Lord, I am staying in agreement with You. I know it's just a matter of time before things change in my favor."

Don't Be Surprised by Opposition

When we were searching for property for a new sanctuary and went to try to acquire the Compaq Center, we had a lot of opposition. After a couple of years, we finally got enough council members to be for us, and we won the vote. We were so excited. We knew God gave us the victory. But three days later, a big real estate company filed a federal lawsuit to try to keep us from moving in. This company was the largest taxpayer in Texas. I had thought the opposition was over, but it was just beginning. Now we had this giant coming against us. They had more resources, more influence, and more experience. I was tempted to get worried and think, *God, what are we going to do? We don't have a chance.* But I had to do what I'm asking you to do. I said, "God, I believe the strength of those coming against us has been cut off. They're bigger, they're stronger, but I know that Your being for us is more than the world being against us."

Like the rose bud that blooms even though it's dead, don't be surprised if you have opposition that blossoms, adversity that blooms, and giants that try to stop you. They look like they have the upper hand. Stay in peace. Their source has been cut off. What you're up against is only temporary. It's just a matter of time before you see the hand of God. When all the odds were against us, it looked as though the Compaq Center could be tied up in the courts for years. We were told the other side would never back down. But out of the blue one day they called and said they wanted to meet. We met with them, and they agreed to not only let us have the building

> *It's just a matter of time before you see the hand of God.*

but to lease us nine thousand covered parking spaces. That two-year legal battle suddenly came to an end.

You may have things you thought were dead—the addiction, the anxiety, the trouble at work, the legal situation—but now they're blossoming, they're getting bigger. You think, *My prayer must not have worked.* No, the roots have been cut off. There may be blooming, but the source is gone. What you're dealing with is only temporary. It can't last without the source. That rose bloom looks so beautiful for a couple of weeks. It seems so alive and looks so permanent, but suddenly it withers. You're about to see some of these "suddenlies." Get ready. That thing you've been praying about, that you believe the roots have been cut off but it seems like it's still alive, is about to wither. The addiction is about to suddenly go. The depression is about to suddenly stop. The opposition is about to suddenly be defeated. The sickness is about to suddenly change. It may be blossoming now, but that's a sign it's on the way out. That's a sign that you're close to your breakthrough. You're close to a new level. You're close to freedom like you've never seen.

Don't be moved by what's temporary. When you walk into someone's house and see a beautiful bouquet of flowers, they look so nice and smell so good. You never think that the flowers are dead. In a few weeks, they'll be thrown out. When negative things are blooming in your life, just like those flowers, they may look vibrant and healthy like they'll be there forever, but you need to remind yourself that they're temporary. The sickness looks really impressive, but I know a secret: It's not going to last. The trouble in your marriage seems so permanent, but this too shall pass. It may seem as though the child who is off course will miss his destiny. No, the source of that trouble has been cut off. It's blooming now, but that doesn't mean it's not dead. There are things you have prayed about that God has already put an end to. The fear is dead. The sickness is dead. The addiction is dead. The

> *Don't be moved by what's temporary.*

poverty is dead. It may take a little time to see it come to pass, but it's on the way. Don't get talked out of it. Don't let what's not happening discourage you. Keep believing, keep thanking God, and you're going to see what God has spoken over your life.

Don't Be Fooled by the Roar

I've heard it said the enemy makes the most noise when he's on the way out. Oftentimes when Jesus told the demons to come out of people, they would let out a loud scream, cause a lot of noise and commotion. Don't panic when the enemy stirs up trouble, when things you thought were dead are blossoming—the sickness looks like it's spreading, your children are acting worse, your finances are getting

> *The enemy makes the most noise when he's on the way out.*

tighter. That's a sign that the enemy is on the way out. He makes the most commotion when he's about to leave.

There was a lady who had a dream in which she was in her house and this very evil-looking person came in. She was watching from over the second floor banister as he started taking her possessions and putting them in a large bag. In the dream she began to pray, saying, "In the name of Jesus I have authority over you. Leave my things alone." The man mocked her and said, "I'm not afraid of you or your prayers." He continued going through the house and taking more of her things. She said again, "You have to go." He laughed and said, "I don't have to leave. Your prayers don't stop me. You don't have any authority over me." But she noticed that while he was saying this, he started putting her things back. He kept mocking her, laughing, causing a commotion, but at the same time he was returning everything he took. This went on until he had put everything back in its proper place. Then he ran out of the house, and she could hear him down the street, still saying, "I'm not afraid of you. You have no authority over me."

The Scripture says, "The enemy goes about like a roaring lion." He's not a lion, but he'll make a lot of noise like one. He'll talk a lot of trash, but his roar doesn't match his bite. Sometimes when we pray, it doesn't seem as though anything is happening. It's as though the enemy is laughing at us, mocking us, saying, "You're not free from this addiction. You'll never get well. Your kids will never get back on track." You have to just stay in faith, keep praying, keep believing. All the time when the enemy's making such a commotion, stirring up trouble, what he won't tell you is that he's putting everything back. He may laugh, but he's putting your children back, he's putting your freedom back, he's putting your finances back, and he's putting your health back.

> *All the time when the enemy's making such a commotion, stirring up trouble, what he won't tell you is that he's putting everything back.*

Don't panic when things get worse, when what you thought was dead looks as though it came back to life. God is still on the throne. He has the final say.

Believe It When You Pray

Jesus says in Mark 11, "Whatever you desire when you pray, believe that you receive it, and you will have it." He doesn't say to believe that you receive it when you see it. He doesn't say to believe when your health turns around or when the breakthrough comes. The key is that you have to believe it happened when you pray. You have to believe it when nothing looks any different. It's when the medical report hasn't improved. It's when your finances haven't turned around. It's when the fig tree looks the same. There's no evidence, but you believe when you prayed that your healing came. You believe when you prayed that your finances turned around. You have to receive it in your spirit before it's going to happen in the natural. You have to be healed in your spirit before you'll see healing in your body. You have to be prosperous in your spirit before you'll be prosperous in the natural.

Too often we believe that we're going to receive it, but we say, "One day I'm going to get well. One day my children are going to do right. One day I'm going to break this addiction." That's going to limit us. The prayer of faith says, "When I pray according to God's Word, I believe it happens right when I pray.

> *The prayer of faith says, "When I pray according to God's Word, I believe it happens right when I pray. I have it in my spirit."*

I have it in my spirit." If you don't receive it in your spirit first, you won't see it in the natural.

When my mother was diagnosed with terminal cancer in 1981, she and my father prayed for healing on December 11. On that day my mother believed she received her healing. She had just been told by the doctors that she had a few weeks to live. Her skin was yellow and she weighed eighty-nine pounds. Nothing in the natural said she was healed. But on that day, she not only prayed but she believed that she received healing. For months nothing looked any different, and she didn't feel any better. It looked as though the cancer was winning, but she kept saying, "Father, thank You that when we prayed on December 11, I received my healing. I believe that day the tide of the battle turned in my health." She kept thanking God, kept calling herself well, and kept declaring healing Scriptures over her life. "I will live and not die. With long life God satisfies me." She started getting better and better. Eventually, she was completely well. The healing she received in her spirit when she wasn't well eventually showed up in her physical body.

When you believe that you receive when you pray, you don't keep asking God to do it. You start thanking Him. If I've already received my healing, I don't have to ask for healing again. I don't have to keep begging God, "Please heal me." Instead, start saying, "Father, thank You that I am healed. Thank You that I am blessed." Maybe you're believing for a scholarship. "Father, I'm asking You for this scholarship. I believe that I receive it right now. I believe it happened." You receive it by faith. From now on, say, "Father, thank You for the scholarship." You just keep thanking God, keep talking like it's going to happen. You may not see anything changing. Every voice says it's never going to work out. That's when you have to dig down deep and say, "I am not going to give up on what God promised me. I'm not going to let negative thoughts talk me out of it. I'm not going to let what's not happening discourage me. I know that what I received in my spirit is on the way."

Don't Lose Your Cows

The writer of Hebrews says, "Hold fast the confession of your faith." You have to hold fast to what God put in your heart. There are forces constantly trying to convince us that what God said is never going to happen. "It's been too long. There's no sign of it. It would have happened by now. Just accept that it's not going to work out." Don't believe those lies. In the unseen realm, things have already changed. The miracle is already in motion. The roots of what's trying to stop you have already been cut off. It's just a matter of time before the manifestation shows up. Now don't get talked out of it. You may be tempted to let it go. You're about to give up on your dream, your healing, your child, or your freedom. No, get a new grip on it. It's closer than you think. You wouldn't be reading this if it wasn't about to happen.

> *There are forces constantly trying to convince us that what God said is never going to happen.*

When I was growing up, my father would hold a big conference at our church every Thanksgiving. It was one of the highlights of the year. He would bring in hundreds of missionaries we support from around the world. For one conference, he decided he wanted to feed everyone at Lakewood. Months before the conference, he prayed and asked God to give him two beef cows so he would have enough meat for all the people. He believed that he received it when he prayed, but week after week went by and there was no sign of any cows. He kept believing, telling the church the cows were on the way, but every thought said, *You're wasting your time. Nobody has ever given you a cow. You better go down to Chick-fil-A and eat more chicken.* As the date got close, thoughts whispered, *You have the money. Just buy the cows. It's not going to happen.* He finally got worn down, quit talking about the cows, and went out and bought the meat for the conference.

A couple of weeks later he had a dream one night in which he saw a huge snake out in a field. He could see the distinct outline of two cows inside that snake. When he woke up, God said to him, "I just want you to know that you let the enemy have your two cows." Those cows already belonged to my father. In the unseen world, they were on the way. But when we quit believing, we get discouraged and say, "I'm never going to get well. The medical report looks just the same. I'll never get out of debt. I'll never meet the right person. Look at the fig tree. It hasn't changed." My message to you is to not lose your cows. What you received in your spirit is en route. It's just a matter of time before it shows up. Hold fast your profession. Keep believing, keep thanking God, keep talking like it's coming.

God is faithful. Don't let the lack of evidence convince you that nothing is happening. In the unseen realm, things are changing in your favor. Forces that have stopped you in the past have been broken. The roots of the depression, the addiction, or the sickness have been cut off. It may look as though it's alive and nothing has changed, but stay in faith. It's just a matter of time and you're going to see what God promised. The reason it's more difficult, the reason it feels as though it's getting worse, is that the enemy is on his way out. I believe and declare that what you received in your spirit is about to show up in the natural. Get ready for promotion, healing, breakthroughs, freedom, the right people, and vindication.

> *Forces that have stopped you in the past have been broken.*

CHAPTER THREE

Your Wings Are Coming

We all face situations that look as though they are permanent. In our career, it seems as though we've reached our limit. We have much bigger things in our spirit, and we know what God promised, but when we look at our bank account, it says we're stuck. When we look at the medical report, or we look at the problem in a relationship, there's no sign of it improving. But the Scripture says, "The things we see are temporary, but the things we can't see are eternal." Don't get discouraged by what you see; it's not permanent. One translation says, "The things we see now are here today, gone tomorrow." That means they are subject to change. Your son may be off course, but he's subject to change. Your health may not be good, but it's subject to change. Your dream may seem impossible, but it's subject to change. Thoughts will tell you, *You'll never get well. You'll never meet the right person.* Instead of being discouraged, turn it around and say, "Yes, it may look that way, but I know a secret: It's subject to change." You can't be moved by what you see; you have to be moved by what you know. God is on the throne. He's working behind the scenes. What He promised will come to pass.

You Weren't Created to Crawl

When a caterpillar is crawling on the ground, barely moving, I can imagine he looks up and sees a beautiful butterfly flying through the air. The more he watches, the more depressed he gets. He thinks, *It's not fair. Why can't I fly? I'll always be grounded. I'm just a glorified worm.* When he looks at his circumstances, there's nothing about them that says he's going to fly. There's no sign of him ever getting off the ground. If an expert examined his body, they would give him no chance of taking flight. He has no wings. You could line him up next to a dozen different worms, and none of them have ever flown. But there's something different about the caterpillar, something that sets him apart from those worms. In its DNA, it's been programmed at a certain time to develop wings. Even though it looks impossible, even though every thought says, *You will never fly,* one day it does the impossible. It turns into a beautiful butterfly and soars through the air. All the time he thought he was permanently stuck on the ground, he didn't realize it was temporary. His wings were coming.

In its DNA, it's been programmed at a certain time to develop wings.

Like that caterpillar, all your circumstances may be telling you that you'll never fly. You don't have the training or the experience, and you don't come from the right family. Thoughts will tell you, *You'll always be grounded. You'll always struggle in your finances. You'll always be addicted.* No, get ready. Your wings are coming. Where you are is not permanent. You weren't created to crawl, to go through life struggling, lonely, or addicted. God didn't make you in His own image, breathe life into you, and crown you with favor so you could barely get by. He created you to soar, to set new standards, to take new ground, to go further than you've imagined.

Now quit being discouraged by what you see. What you see is subject to change. You don't know what God is up to. You don't know what He's doing behind the scenes. It would be different if a caterpillar

> *God didn't make you in His own image, breathe life into you, and crown you with favor so you could barely get by.*

was born with wings that didn't work but eventually they were activated. You could see the wings and think, *One day it's coming.* It would be much easier to believe that it was going to fly if the wings were already in place. But I believe one reason God made the caterpillar stage with no wings, that crawls on the ground, that's the least likely one to fly, was to encourage us. I believe that when it seems the least likely for you to fly, when the circumstances say

there's no way for you to get well, no way to get out of debt, no way to accomplish your dream, He wants you to remember the caterpillar. If the caterpillar can go from being grounded, without wings, to being a beautiful butterfly soaring through the air, then God can change what looks impossible for us. You may be in the caterpillar stage now, not making much progress, and things don't look very promising. God is

> *If the caterpillar can go from being grounded, without wings, to being a beautiful butterfly soaring through the air, then God can change what looks impossible for us.*

saying, "Don't worry. Your wings are coming. Your healing is coming. Your promotion is coming. Your breakthrough is coming." You're not going to just get ahead or just get a bump. You're going to see supernatural increase, supernatural opportunity, things you couldn't make happen.

When a caterpillar transforms into a butterfly and gets his wings, it doesn't have the ability to crawl faster, to just do better at what it could already do. No, it comes into a whole new dimension—from crawling to flying. When you get your wings, you're not just going to do a little better at what you're doing. God is going to catapult you into a new dimension, into favor like you've never seen. It's acceleration. Things that should have taken you years are going to happen in a fraction of the time. It should have taken you thirty years to work your way up in the company, but suddenly you are promoted. What happened? You got your wings. It should have taken you a lifetime to pay your house off or to get out of debt, but you did it in a fraction of the time. You got your wings. You went from crawling to flying. That's the hand of God thrusting you ahead.

That's what happened to us at Lakewood. We were doing great at our old location. We were blessed and growing, but things exploded when we moved into the Compaq Center in 2005. We didn't just go to a new level, we went to a new dimension. We got our wings. The building put us fifty years down the road. What am I saying? Your idea of flying and God's idea of flying are totally different. You think you're doing well now, but wait until you get your wings. You haven't seen, heard, or imagined what God has in store. He's going to open doors you never dreamed would open. He's going to bring people strategically into your life, divine connections, who will use their influence to push you ahead. You're not going to have to find them; they're going to find you. You're going to discover talent, creativity, and ideas that you hadn't known you had.

> *Your idea of flying and God's idea of flying are totally different.*

You're going to think, *Where did I get this?* You got your wings.

That's God causing you to go places that you could never go on your own.

What You Hear Versus What You See

In 1 Kings 18, the people of Samaria were in a great drought. It hadn't rained in three years, their crops had dried up, and they were barely surviving. The prophet Elijah showed up and said to King Ahab, "I hear the sound of the abundance of rain." When he said that, there wasn't a cloud in the sky. There wasn't any sign of rain, yet he chose to believe what he heard in his spirit over what he saw with his eyes. He saw drought, famine, and dried-up crops, but he heard an abundance of rain. Are you believing what you're seeing or what you're hearing? What you see may be lack, struggle, a caterpillar crawling on the ground, but what God is speaking to your spirit is abundance, healing, breakthroughs, and new levels. What you're hearing is more powerful than what you're seeing. What you see is temporary; what you're hearing is eternal. If you're focusing on the drought, how big the obstacle is, how long it's been, that's going to keep you in a caterpillar stage.

The apostle Paul says in Romans 12, "Be transformed by the renewing of your mind." The word *transformed* is the same word used for when caterpillars *metamorphose* into butterflies. You have to get your mind going in the right direction. You can't think caterpillar thoughts and live a butterfly life. If you think, *I'll never get well. I can't get ahead. I've reached my limits*, your own thinking is going to keep your wings from developing. You have to do as Elijah did. Everywhere he looked he saw drought, but in his spirit he heard abundance. He had to choose whether he was going to agree with

> *You can't think caterpillar thoughts and live a butterfly life.*

what he saw or with what he heard. He chose to believe what God said over what he saw. Everything you see may contradict what you hear, but you have to walk by faith, not by sight. That's what faith is all about.

After Elijah told King Ahab that he heard the sound of an abundance of rain, he climbed to the top of Mount Carmel. He told his assistant to go up and look toward the sea and see if there was any sign of rain. The man went, came back, and said. "There's not a cloud in the sky." Elijah could have gotten discouraged and thought he must have heard God wrong. But he understood this principle that what he saw was subject to change. Instead of accept-

> *You have to be more confident in what God says than in what you see.*

ing that it wasn't going to happen, he told his assistant to go up and look again. The man came back and said there was still no sign of rain. Elijah told him to go back and look again and again and again. It takes faith to keep looking. The medical report may not be good, but go back and look again. If it isn't good the next time, go look again. You have to be more confident in what God says than in what you see.

What you see may be a wingless caterpillar, with no chance that you can fly. Thoughts will tell you that you're wasting your time if you're waiting to see how you're going to get off the ground. Some people will tell you that your faith makes you look foolish and you're not thinking straight. But faith is not always going to make sense. What God promised you is not always going to be logical. There will be a battle taking place in your mind between what you see and what you hear. "I know I'm a butterfly. I know I'm created to soar. I know I'm going to do great things." But the other voice says, "Where are your wings? Why are you crawling? Where are all the good breaks? How could it happen?" You're right where Elijah was. "God, You said there's an abundance of rain, but I don't even see a cloud. God, if it's true, at least give me a little drizzle. At least let the weatherman say ten percent chance of rain. Give me a little encouragement."

Sometimes you won't see any sign that it's going to happen. That's when you have to dig down deep and say, "God, my mind says I'm crazy, and people think I'm far out. But I believe that what You promised is still on the way. You say that You will restore health to me. I don't see any sign of it, but I choose to believe healing is coming. My child is off course, but Your Word says, 'as for me and my house, we will serve the Lord.' I'm not going to be moved by what I see. I know that You have the final say. God, You say I will prosper and succeed, that I will leave an inheritance to my children's children. I'm struggling to make ends meet, and I don't see how it can happen, but I believe my wings are coming. I hear abundance in my spirit. I hear increase. I hear that I will lend and not borrow."

The seventh time that Elijah's assistant came back, he said, "This time I see a small cloud rising from the sea, the size of a man's hand." Elijah sent word to Ahab: "You better hitch up your chariot and head for the next city. There's about to be a downpour." All he saw was a little cloud, but he was so full of faith, so full of expectancy, that he knew that small cloud was about to turn into a big rain. It wasn't long until the sky grew black with clouds, a huge downpour fell, and the three-year drought came to an end. What you see may seem small compared to what God promised you. It's easy to dismiss it and think it's nothing. But God can take a small

> *God can take a small cloud and bring a big blessing.*

cloud and bring a big blessing. He can take what looks insignificant and cause it to explode into something amazing.

The Cocoon Is Where You Transform

I wonder if Elijah would have ever seen the rain if he had not kept looking. If he had gotten discouraged after the first time, or the third time, or the sixth time, maybe the cloud wouldn't have formed. Maybe God was seeing how badly he wanted it. Maybe the clear skies and no clouds were all a test. Perhaps God was saying, "Are you going to believe what I say over what you see? Are you going to believe your wings are coming while you're still crawling on the ground, while there is no sign of it? Or are you going to let the circumstances talk you out of it?" What you decide is going to determine what happens.

Sometimes part of the test is that the situation will get worse before it gets better. Elijah did all the right things. In the face of the drought, with all the odds against him, he declared to Ahab what God said, that the abundance of rain was coming. He went up on the mountain and prayed. He thanked God in advance, and he looked for it with expectancy, but nothing changed—no clouds, no rain. Here he's doing everything he's supposed to be doing, but the drought got worse. If you stay in faith and pass this test of things getting worse when you're doing the right thing, you will come into abundance as Elijah did. You'll see what God promised. The getting worse is a sign the breakthrough is coming.

> *The getting worse is a sign the breakthrough is coming.*

It's the same with the caterpillar. Before the wings are formed, the caterpillar goes into a cocoon. That's where it transforms. In the cocoon it's dark, he can't move, and it's uncomfortable. At least when he was a caterpillar, he could crawl. He couldn't go fast, but he could move. Now he's restricted. I'm sure he thinks, *What's happening to me? I was believing for wings. I was hoping to fly. Now I have no mobility. It's worse than ever.* In a little while, after that dark season, after it's uncomfortable, he comes out of the cocoon, but he is not the same. Now he's a butterfly, with wings. Now he can fly. Maybe you're in the cocoon now, and you feel as though you've gone backward. You were believing to get better, but it's gone the other way. You're uncomfortable, and you're wondering, *What's happening? What did I do wrong?* It's all a part of the process. That's a sign your wings are coming. That's a sign those clouds are forming. Don't get discouraged. You're about to come into who you were created to be.

The time in the cocoon, the uncomfortable season when you're doing the right thing and the wrong thing is happening, isn't a mistake. It isn't bad luck. It's a test. God has you in the palms of His hands, and nothing can happen to you without His permission. Because you stay in faith, because you keep looking for the cloud, because you keep declaring abundance is coming, you're going to come out with your wings. No more crawling. No more barely making it, struggling with addictions and dysfunction.

> *Because you stay in faith, because you keep looking for the cloud, because you keep declaring abundance is coming, you're going to come out with your wings.*

It's a new day. If the enemy had known what was going to happen, he would have left you alone. He thought he was taking you into that difficult time, into that loss, into that disappointment to stop you. He didn't realize that it was the cocoon. God was using it to transform you. You came out with your wings. Now you can fly. Now you can take new ground. Now abundance is in your future.

It's Subject to Change

In the previous chapter, I mentioned briefly that when we went to acquire the Compaq Center, we faced nearly two years of opposition. But in December 2002, the Houston City Council voted for us to have the property. It was a dream come true. However, a few days later, the gigantic real estate company that owned all the property around the Compaq Center filed a federal lawsuit stating that we were in violation of the deed restrictions. The lawsuit blocked us from taking possession and moving in. We met with our attorneys, who weren't very encouraging. They said we could possibly win, but even if we did, it could be tied up in the courts for ten years. Month after month passed. Nothing was happening. They weren't going to budge.

I had to do what I'm asking you to do. I said, "God, I'm not going to be moved by what I see. What I see is Goliath. What I see is a stalemate. What I see is a lengthy legal battle." It looked as though we were going to stay grounded. It looked as though the setback was permanent. But I knew a secret: It was subject to change. People don't have the final say; God has the final say. Instead of talking about how bad it looked, and how big the opponents were, I went around saying, "Father, thank You that Your being for us is more than the world being against us. I may not see a way, but I know You have a way."

After two years, we received word that the CEO of this large company wanted to meet with us. Our attorneys told us not to get our hopes up, that it was probably a ploy, a negotiating tactic to try to intimidate and pressure us. They expected the worst, but deep down I believed it was the hand of God. We'd had no contact with them except through the courts. When the CEO walked into the boardroom, the first thing he said was, "Joel, I watch you every week on television, and my

> *God knows how to put the right people in your path.*

son-in-law is a youth pastor." God knows how to put the right people in your path. By the end of the day, they had agreed to not only drop the lawsuit and let us have the building, but to lease us nine thousand covered parking spaces that surround this building. It looked as though we were grounded, but God gave us our wings. It could have taken ten years, but it happened in a fraction of the time.

What you're up against may seem bigger and stronger. When the odds are against you, don't worry. The Most High God is for you. He knows how to defeat the giants. He knows how to turn things around. No person can stand against Him. No sickness, no addiction, and no obstacle can hold you back. Whatever is trying to stop you is subject to change. It may look permanent, but it's only temporary.

> *Don't be moved by what you see; be moved by what you know.*

Don't be moved by what you see; be moved by what you know. God is working behind the scenes right now, making your crooked places straight, pushing back the forces of darkness, changing people's minds in your favor. Not only are you going to come out, but in the process you're going to discover your wings. You're going to rise to levels you never dreamed.

Don't Reduce What God Promised

In the Scripture, God promised Abraham and Sarah that they were going to have a baby, but they were both way too old. Even though it seemed impossible, they believed for a while, but years went by with no sign of a baby. Finally, Sarah told Abraham to sleep with her maid. Her attitude was: *I'll never get my wings. I'll always be grounded.* She thought that someone else would have to fly for her, and that she would have to ride piggyback. "They" would have the child. But you never see a butterfly flying around with a caterpillar on its back. The promise that God put in you is not going to come through someone else. Yes, sometimes people lift us, sometimes they do us favors, but God didn't create you to be dependent on others to fulfill your destiny. You're not going to have to ride piggyback. Your wings are coming. There is greatness in you—gifts, talents, children, businesses—that is going to come out.

> *You're not going to have to ride piggyback. Your wings are coming.*

Abraham had a baby with Sarah's maid, but he wasn't the promised child. You may settle, but God is not going to settle. When it seemed as though there was no way, God stepped in and said, "I know this looks impossible. I know Sarah has been barren for her whole life, but this is subject to change." Against all odds, at ninety years old, Sarah gave birth to a son, the promised child. What God put in your heart is still on the way. Maybe the reason it seems so unlikely is because you don't have your wings yet. When you're in the caterpillar stage, it's easy to talk yourself out of it. The way you stay in faith is to remind yourself, "My wings are coming."

When Sarah heard the promise that she was going to have a

baby, the first thing she did was laugh. She thought, *That's so far out, it's funny.* Because she couldn't comprehend it before, she had put forward her maid to try to make it happen. Here's a key: Don't reduce what God's promised you to fit your faith. Don't bring it down to your level and go find the maid, so to speak. Come up to His level. Don't be limited by your faith. Stretch your faith. If you can do it on your own, you don't need your wings. If you can accomplish your dreams by yourself, it doesn't take faith. What God has in your future is so big, so amazing, that it's going to be intimidating. While you're excited, you'll also be tempted to think, *There's no way. That's never happened in my family. I don't see how I could get well. How can I break this addiction? How can I run this business?* God wouldn't have given it to you if He didn't have a way to bring it to pass. He's not asking you to figure it out. He's asking you to believe. When you believe, supernatural doors will open. When you believe, God will make things happen that you couldn't make happen.

But too often we make the mistake of reducing what God promised us to what we think is possible. A young couple came for prayer one time and said, "Joel, will you pray that the furniture we really want to buy will go on sale so we can afford it?" There's nothing wrong with being frugal, and I'm all for getting good deals. But God is not depending on what someone else does to bring your dream to pass. He's not hoping they'll give you a good break so that promise will be fulfilled. I told the couple, "That's great if it goes on sale. But I'd rather pray that God will give you the funds, so even if it doesn't go on sale, you'll be able to purchase it." Sometimes we're praying for things to come down when we should be praying for us to go up. The same God who

> *Sometimes we're praying for things to come down when we should be praying for us to go up.*

can cause it to go on sale can also bless you in such a way that even if it doesn't, you still have plenty to buy it.

No More Worm Mentality

My father was raised in poverty, never had enough food, and went to school with holes in his shoes. When I was ten years old, we were in a clothing store and my dad was about to buy a suit. When the salesman found out he was a pastor, he said, "Let me go check and see if I can get you a minister's discount." My father was very frugal, but something about that hit him wrong. He said, "I appreciate your checking, but that won't be necessary. My Father is very wealthy." The salesman gave him a surprised look. He didn't know that my father was talking about his Heavenly Father. My father's attitude was: *I was grounded long enough. I crawled around for years, but this is a new day. I have my wings, and I'm not going back to a worm mentality. I was born to fly.* Sometimes when we're waiting for God to bring us up higher, God is waiting for us to bring our thinking up higher. Get rid of that worm mentality. Don't reduce what God put in your spirit to fit your faith.

> Sometimes when we're waiting for God to bring us up higher, God is waiting for us to bring our thinking up higher.

Stretch your faith. How you were raised is not how you're supposed to stay. What you've seen in the past is not your destiny. God has new levels.

You may not see how something can happen because there are big obstacles in your path. Don't be moved by what you see. What you see is subject to change. As with Elijah, I hear the sound of abundance. I hear the sound of increase, the sound of break-throughs, the sound of healing. You may have been grounded, but I have good news. Your caterpillar days are over. I believe and declare that your wings are coming. God is about to take you higher. You're going to accomplish more than you thought pos-sible. It's going to happen faster than you think, with new levels, breakthroughs, and the fullness of your destiny.

CHAPTER FOUR

The Promise Is Coming

As we go through life, we all have things we're believing for, dreams God put in our heart, and problems to turn around. But when it's been so long, when we've made mistakes and people have come against us, all the circumstances say, "There's no way. If it was going to happen, it would have happened by now." It's easy to get discouraged and accept that it's never going to work out. But what God promised you doesn't have an expiration date. Just because you've given up on it doesn't mean God has given up. You may have done things that should keep your dream from coming to pass. Perhaps you got off course and made mistakes. You don't deserve for it to happen, but God is so merciful that He's already taken your mistakes into account. They may delay it from happening, but they're not going to deny it from happening. The promise is still coming. Despite the mistakes, despite the failures, despite the delays, God is saying, "I'm still going to bless you. I'm still going to heal you. I'm still going to bring that dream to pass."

> *What God promised you doesn't have an expiration date.*

Too often we disqualify ourselves. We think it would have

> *The good news is that He has mercy for every mistake, restoration for every failure, new beginnings for every loss, a comeback for every setback.*

happened if we had made better choices. If we'd finished school, if we'd not got involved with the wrong people, not wasted time compromising, then God could bless us, then He would open new doors. That would make sense if God was like us. That would make sense if He judged us based on our performance and gave us what we deserve. But God is not like that. He's full of mercy. He doesn't hold our mistakes against us. He doesn't cancel our destiny because we got off course. He knew every wrong turn we would take, every mess we would make, every failure, every weakness. Nothing you've done is a surprise to God. Nothing that's happened to you has caught Him off guard. The good news is that He has mercy for every mistake, restoration for every failure, new beginnings for every loss, a comeback for every setback. What He promised you is still on the way.

You didn't miss your chance. You haven't failed too many times. The disappointment didn't stop God's plan. He is still going to show you favor. The circumstances may look impossible. The medical report tells you to learn to live with the sickness. It's permanent. But God says, "Healing is coming. Wholeness is coming. The number of your days I will fulfill." You may not see how you can ever get out of debt. Nobody in your family has excelled, but it can start with you. God says, "Increase is coming. Abundance is coming. You will lend and not borrow. What you touch will prosper and succeed." You may say, "Joel, I got myself into this mess. It's my own fault." But God is the one who's going to get you out of that mess.

Quit believing the lies that it's too late, that the problem is too big, that you've made too many mistakes. God is called "the author and the finisher of your faith." What He started, He's going to finish. The delay doesn't mean it's not going to happen. The mistakes you've made haven't caused God to change His mind. The circumstances may look impossible, but God hasn't run out of options. You may not see a way in the natural, but God is supernatural. He has ways you've never thought of. He's not limited by your job, by your salary, by a medical report, by what family you come from, or by what you didn't get. One touch of His favor will catapult you to a new level. One good break and what He promised you will come to pass. Instead of thinking of all the reasons why it's not going to work out, all through the day you have to say, "Father, thank You that what

> *The circumstances may look impossible, but God hasn't run out of options.*

You promised is on the way. Thank You that healing is on the way. Thank You that promotion is on the way. Thank You that the right person, breakthroughs, freedom, and new levels are on the way."

Don't Try to Help God Out

In the previous chapter, I introduced the story of how God told Abraham that he and his wife, Sarah, were going to have a baby. Abraham was seventy-five years old, and Sarah was sixty-five. They had been married for years and not had any children. This seemed impossi-

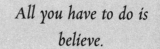

> *All you have to do is believe.*

ble. They were too old. Sometimes God will put promises in your heart that don't make sense to your mind. He'll put bigger things in your spirit than you think you can accomplish on your own. The key is to let it take root in your heart. You don't have to figure it out. You don't have to come up with how it's going to happen. All you have to do is believe.

Years went by, and Abraham and Sarah didn't have a baby, so they tried to help God out. Sarah told Abraham to sleep with her maid Hagar, thinking that she could build a family through Hagar. They had a son they named Ishmael, but Ishmael wasn't the promised child. That's what the Scripture calls "the works of the flesh." That's when we try to make things happen in our own way, in our own strength, in our own timing. Abraham loved Ishmael, but Ishmael became a constant source of conflict. When tensions arose between Sarah and Hagar, Sarah got mad at Abraham for having slept with Hagar. There was strife and division. She finally treated Hagar so badly that Hagar fled into the desert, though she did return. Years later, it got so bad that Sarah gave Abraham an ultimatum that Hagar and Ishmael had to leave for good. Abraham was torn, but God reassured him that they would be okay, so he sent them away. It had all been a big mess, with all kinds of dysfunction.

For thirteen years God was silent. Abraham didn't hear anything. I'm sure thoughts told him, *You blew it. You made a big mess. You had a baby with another woman. The promised child is never going to happen now.* But just because God is silent doesn't mean He's given up. You may have delayed the promise, but that didn't deny it. God didn't change His mind. Will you trust Him in the seasons of silence? Every thought may tell you, *It's never going to happen. It's your own fault. You knew better.* You may not see anything happening, but God is still working. What He promised you is still on the way.

> *Will you trust Him in the seasons of silence?*

After thirteen years of silence, when Abraham was ninety-nine, it says in Genesis 17, "God said to Abraham, 'I am God Almighty. You will become the father of many nations.'" After all the mistakes, all the failures, and all the dysfunction, the first thing God said was, "Abraham, you will become a father with Sarah." He reminded Abraham of the promise. He was saying, "Even though you blew it, even though you made a mess, that didn't stop My plan. I didn't change My mind. I'm still going to do what I promised." You would think the first thing God would say was, "Abraham, I'm disappointed in you. What were you thinking? I'm going to find somebody else to accomplish your destiny." God never gives up on you. He never disqualifies you. Quit disqualifying yourself. You blew it? Join the crowd. We all have. You made a mess? Come on in. You're in good company. The enemy is called "the accuser of the brethren." He'll remind you of everything you've done wrong, all the mistakes you've made. He'd love to convince you to live down on yourself and drag through life with no passion, no expectancy. Don't fall into that trap.

At ninety years old, Sarah conceived and gave birth to a son they named Isaac, the promised child. The Scripture says, "It happened at the exact time God said it would." That tells me that God already knew they were going to make those mistakes. He knew they would be impatient and have the first son and get into strife. Isaac came right on schedule, right when God had planned. Are you believing the lies that you've missed your chance, that it's too late? Are you believing that if you would have made better

> *Are you believing that if you would have made better choices, if you would have been more disciplined, if you had not run around with the people who pulled you down, then the promise would have been yours?*

choices, if you would have been more disciplined, if you had not run around with the people who pulled you down, then the promise would have been yours? What happened in the past is not a surprise to God. What He promised you is right on schedule. You didn't miss it; it's still in your future.

It's Coming Right On Schedule

I talked to an older gentleman who struggled with drugs and alcohol for most of his life. He was raised in a good home with a single mother, but they lived in a rough environment where he got involved with the wrong crowd. He had gone to rehab again and again, which worked for a while but he always fell back. His own thoughts not only told him how bad he was, but the people around him were constantly putting him down and making him feel like a failure. He got so down on himself that he came to the place where he didn't want to live. But then he turned on the television one day and started watching our program. He said, "Joel, everybody told me how bad I was, how I was a failure, how I hadn't done anything with my life. But you were the first one to tell me how good I was, and how I was made in the image of God." He'd never had anyone speak life into him and tell him what he could become. When he heard me say, "You are a child of the Most High God," something came alive inside.

This man got down on his knees and said, "God, I've made a mess of my life. I've tried to clean up on my own, but I can't do this by myself. Please help me to change." From that moment on, he never had the desire for the drugs, and he never touched alcohol again. Today, he works in the prisons, encouraging the inmates, letting them know that they too are children of the Most

High God. You may have failed but you are not a failure. Failure is an event; it's not who you are. You may have an addiction, but you are not

> *What you struggle with is not who you are.*

an addict. What you struggle with is not who you are. What you do may not be good, but you are good. The Creator of the universe breathed life into you. As with this man, you may have gotten off course and brought the trouble on yourself, but God is saying, "I'm still going to bless you. I'm still going to free you. I'm still going to use you to help others. I'm still going to show you My favor."

Jesus says in Matthew 5, "You are blessed when you're at the end of your rope. With less of you, there's more of God and His rule." That means there is more of His favor, His healing, His freedom. Abraham was at the end of his rope in the natural, but God showed up and gave him the promised child. This man was at the end of his rope, addicted for years, but God showed up and brought freedom. You may be facing a medical situation that doesn't look good, or something in your finances, something in a relationship, or something in your business is at the end of the rope. You don't know how it's going to work out, how it's going to make it. Have a new perspective. When you're at the end, it's a blessing in disguise. You're in prime position for God to show out in your life. He's saying to you what He said to Abraham: "I am God Almighty. What I promised you is still on the way." Those dreams you've given up on are still on the way. The healing you're praying about is on the way. The freedom, the right person, or the baby you've been believing for is on the way.

Instead of being down on yourself, going around discouraged, turn it around and say, "Father, thank You that You are the Almighty God. Your mercy is bigger than my mistakes. You are greater than this sickness. You are more powerful than this addiction. Even though I'm in a season of silence, even though I don't see anything happening, I know You're working behind the scenes and what You promised me is right on schedule."

When You Don't Have What You Need

Think about Abraham. At ninety-nine years old, he didn't have the seed for a child. Even if Sarah could conceive, even if somehow her womb was fertile, without the seed it wouldn't happen. Abraham could have thought, *God, I could believe we would have a baby if I had the seed, but the problem is that I'm lacking. I don't have what I need.* You may feel as though you're lacking in some area—lacking talent, lacking experience, lacking finances, lacking support. God knows what you don't have. He knows what's in your bank account, He knows who's not for you, and He knows what the medical report says. The good news is that He's going to make up for what you don't have. He gave Abraham the seed for a child, and little Isaac was born. Forty-two generations later, a young virgin named Mary gave birth to Jesus. The book of Galatians refers to Jesus as "the seed of Abraham."

God could have caused Abraham to have a baby when he was younger, when he still had the ability. It's interesting that God waited until he didn't have the seed. Sometimes God will let you run out of what you need on purpose so you have to depend on Him. It's when your only option is, "God, if You don't do this, it's not going to happen. If You don't open the door, if You don't turn my child around, if You don't heal my body, then it's over." That's what Jesus

> *Sometimes God will let you run out of what you need on purpose so you have to depend on Him.*

was saying: "When you're at the end of your ability, then there's room for God's favor, there's room for Him to show out."

If Abraham were here today, he would tell you to not let the circumstances fool you. Don't let what you don't have talk you out of what's in your heart. Don't let your mistakes, your failures, the delays, or the seasons of silence cause you to think it's never going to happen. The Lord God Almighty is going to do for you what He did for Abraham. He's going to bless you in spite of your mistakes. He's going to promote you in spite of the odds being against you. He's going to make things happen that you didn't deserve, you didn't work for, and you didn't see coming. It's just the goodness and mercy of God. What He promised is still on the way.

Be Patient

Years ago, there was a business venture that came across my path. It seemed like a once-in-a-lifetime opportunity. I was so excited that I didn't even have to pray about it or think twice about it. This was too good to be true. I just said yes. Along the way, as we were researching it more and talking with some experts, there were some red flags, things that didn't add up. But I was so set on having my way that I overlooked it, didn't pay any attention. We signed the contract, got it up and going, but it wasn't what I thought. Things didn't take off as we planned. There were some limitations that we didn't realize and setbacks that we didn't anticipate. It was a constant struggle, a financial burden. I didn't know how it was going to turn out. I had taken on this big obligation, but I was in over my head, and it was nobody's fault except my own. I knew that God put big things in my heart, but I was impatient like Abraham. I tried to make it happen in my own strength.

In Psalm 106, the psalmist says, "The Israelites did not wait for God's plan to unfold." It's easy to get in a hurry and try to make things happen, to force doors to open, to manipulate people and circumstances. If you push hard enough, sometimes God will let you open a door that He hasn't ordained. He'll let you walk down a road that's not His best path. I'm all for taking risks and getting out of our comfort zone, but it's important to stay in God's timing. You have to listen to that still small voice inside. An opportunity may be right for you, but if you feel an unrest about it, it might not be the right timing. Abraham knew that God promised him a baby, but God never said the child would come through Hagar. When it wasn't happening on their timetable, when it was taking longer than they thought it should, they stepped in and decided to help God out. Abraham had a baby, but not the child of promise. God doesn't need your help in that way.

> *If you push hard enough, sometimes God will let you open a door that He hasn't ordained.*

My business venture never got off the ground, but here's how good God is. Even though I made the mess, even though I overrode what I was feeling and brought this trouble on myself, God supernaturally turned it around, and we came out of it way better than we went into it. It ended up being a huge blessing. God took that mistake and turned it into a miracle. That's the mercy of God. When we don't deserve it, we made mistakes, we got in a hurry, God says, "I'm still going to bless you. I'm still going to favor you. I'm still going to get you to where you're supposed to be." Quit beating yourself up. Quit believing the lies that you've seen your best days, that it's too late to accomplish your dreams, that you can never

> *Start believing again. Start dreaming again. Start making plans for what you've given up on.*

get out of debt, that you've made too many bad choices. What God promised you is still on the way. You may have delayed it, but you didn't deny it. It's still on the schedule. Start believing again. Start dreaming again. Start making plans for what you've given up on.

I met a young couple who had been trying to have a baby for eleven years. When they came for prayer during a service, the lady was weeping and weeping. She wanted to have a baby so badly, but all the medical reports said there was no way. They had taken fertility treatments and done everything they could. Against all odds, they conceived and gave birth to a beautiful baby girl. Medically speaking, it was impossible, but when the Lord God Almighty shows up, what's impossible becomes possible. What He's destined for your life will come to pass. Once she was weeping with tears of sadness, so heartbroken, but at the service for their baby's dedication she was weeping with tears of joy, so overwhelmed with God's goodness.

You may have shed some tears of sadness over what hasn't worked out, over dreams that haven't come to pass, over disappointments and loss. As with her, God is going to turn your mourning into dancing, those tears of sorrow into tears of joy. It may not have happened yet, but it's not over. The psalmist says, "Weeping may endure for a night, but joy comes in the morning." Your morning is coming. Your baby is coming. Your healing is coming. Your spouse is coming. Your breakthrough is coming. When it happens, it's going to be more rewarding, more fulfilling than you ever imagined.

Through a Season of Silence

Moses was born into a Hebrew family, but he was raised by Egyptians. When he was a young man, God gave him a dream that he would deliver the Israelites out of slavery in Egypt. One day when he saw an Egyptian foreman beating a Hebrew slave, he didn't think anyone was watching and he killed the foreman. His intentions were good, but he got out of God's timing. He didn't wait for the plan to unfold. When the word got out about what Moses had done, he had to run for his life. He spent forty years hiding in the backside of the desert. Here he had a call on his life, he knew what God promised him, but he blew it. It was his own fault. I'm sure he lived with regrets. There weren't many days when he didn't think about that mistake. *Why didn't I use better judgment? Why didn't I keep my cool?* It looked as though that one act had canceled the promise, but God doesn't change His mind.

> *God uses the delays and the setbacks to develop us, to get us prepared for where He's taking us. Nothing is wasted.*

Our mistakes may delay them, but even then God uses the delays and the setbacks to develop us, to get us prepared for where He's taking us. Nothing is wasted. If you keep the right attitude, all things will work for your good.

One morning while Moses was in the wilderness tending sheep, a bush suddenly exploded into flames and caught fire. He'd probably seen spontaneous combustion out there before, but what made this unique was that the bush didn't burn up. He was so intrigued that he went over to it, and a voice boomed out, "Moses! Moses! Take off your sandals, for you are standing on holy ground." It had been forty years since he'd heard God's voice. The season of silence had been so long that he thought God had forgotten about him. He'd already accepted that he had missed his destiny. But at eighty years old, after his mistakes, after his failures, Moses heard God say, "Now I'm ready for you to go deliver the Israelites." Moses went and did just that.

As with Moses, you may have made mistakes and gone through setbacks, and you don't think you can ever accomplish what's in your heart. It's been too long. But that season of silence doesn't mean God has forgotten about you. During those forty years that Moses was in the desert, the Scripture says he became the most humble man on the face of the Earth. God is working on you in the silent years. You may not realize it, but He's getting you prepared. Your time is coming. Your burning bush is on the way. What God started, He's still going to bring to pass. Even when it's your fault, He's still going to bless you. He's still going to show you favor. He's still going to open doors that you couldn't open.

> *God is working on you in the silent years.*

Mistakes Turned into Miracles

I talked to a man who was seventeen years old when he got his girlfriend pregnant back in the 1960s. Their parents were not happy. His parents sent him off to the Marine Corps, and the young lady and her family moved to another state. While he was in boot camp, his girlfriend informed him that she was giving the child up for adoption. He went overseas to serve in the Special Forces. He hoped that he and his girlfriend would get together when he returned home, but she sent him a letter saying she was moving on. They went their separate ways, and both eventually got married to other people. In 2009, the man's wife of twenty-four years died from cancer. He was heartbroken. Three months later, he received a sympathy card in the mail from his former girlfriend. They hadn't communicated with each other in forty-two years. She wrote that her husband had passed as well.

This man was able to find her phone number and call her. They couldn't believe they were talking with each other after all those years. On top of that, the lady told him that she had just found their daughter whom she had given up for adoption. Their daughter lived a few minutes from her. The man went to see the lady, and he met his daughter for the first time, as well as his ten-year-old grandson. It was like a dream come true. He and the lady started dating. A year later, they were married, with their daughter as the maid of honor.

God knows how to take mistakes we've made and turn them into miracles. It's not too late. You haven't missed your chance, and you don't know what God is up to. He can make things happen that you never dreamed would happen. I'm sure that Moses thought he'd never fulfill his destiny. Abraham never thought he'd see that baby and become the father of many nations. This man never thought he'd meet his daughter and see his family restored. But God is full of mercy. There are promises you may have given up on, but God hasn't given up. They're still in your future. Don't go around down on yourself, thinking you've seen your best days. Stir up your faith. The Lord God Almighty is at work in your life right now. I believe and declare that what He promised is still going to come to pass. Your Isaac is on the way.

> *He can make things happen that you never dreamed would happen.*

CHAPTER FIVE

The Shaking Is for Shifting

When the coronavirus pandemic hit, it was something we'd never experienced. The world economy was shaken, and so many people could not go to work. Our social lives were shaken, and we were forced to stay apart. With all the fear and uncertainty, many people's emotional well-being was shaken. In life, we all have these times when things shake us to our core. It might be an unexpected illness, or we lose a loved one, or we've been at a workplace for years but now there's opposition, people who are trying to push us out. Suddenly the stability we were used to, or the children doing great things, or the finances we were counting on, are no longer there. It's easy to get discouraged and wonder why it happened. But here's the key: The shaking is not there to stop you; the shaking is there to shift you. If you keep the right attitude, the shaking will shift you into promotion, shift you into greater influence, shift you into better relationships. God uses the shakings to get us in position for new levels.

> *The shaking is not there to stop you; the shaking is there to shift you.*

Without the door closing, we would never get out of our comfort zone. We may not like it, but the shaking is forcing us to

> *If everything kept going along as usual, we would never reach our potential.*

change, forcing us to grow. If everything kept going along as usual, we would never reach our potential. Stay open for something new. Don't go back to the same ways you used to do things. The reason God allowed the shaking is to shift you into something better. If your company had to furlough you, that wasn't a surprise to God. He shook things up so He could give you a better position, with better benefits, in a better environment. It looks like a setback, but it's really a setup. God is using it to shift you to where you couldn't go on your own.

When Your World Is Turned Upside Down

In Acts 2, the disciples were in the upper room when the Holy Spirit came in like a rushing mighty wind. They were all filled with the Spirit. They knew that God was with them and they were going to do great things. But in Acts 8, a man named Saul came along who hated the disciples. He had letters from the authorities to have them arrested and put in jail. The Scripture says, "Saul wreaked havoc on the church in Jerusalem." Here the disciples had been going along fine, seeing God's favor and blessing, and out of nowhere Saul showed up and turned things upside down. Their whole world was shaken. It's interesting that Saul came to Jerusalem and caused so much turmoil. Jerusalem means "the city of peace." This was home for many of the early disciples. This was where they felt secure. They could relax and be comfortable. But now this city of peace was the city of chaos.

I'm sure they thought, *God, where are You? Don't You see what*

Saul is doing? Do You see how much trouble we're in? Just a few chapters earlier, God had sent the rushing mighty wind. It wasn't as though He couldn't have stopped Saul. He parted the Red Sea and closed the mouths of lions. He could have kept Saul from ever entering Jerusalem. He could have sent angels to hold him back. But sometimes God will allow things to be shaken. He'll allow a Saul, a difficulty, an unfair situation to shake us. You have to understand that the shaking is not there to stop you but to shift you. It's getting you into position to go to a new level, to see things you've never seen, and then you'll not live worried, upset, wondering how it's going to work out. Anyone can trust God when things are going their way, when life is good, when you're seeing favor. The real test is, Will you trust Him when things are shaking? Will you stay in faith when there's uncertainty, when there are things you don't understand?

> *The real test is, Will you trust Him when things are shaking?*

God has you in the palms of His hands. Nothing can happen to you without His permission. Something or someone may have wreaked havoc in your life, and things may feel as though they're out of control. Can I encourage you that God is still on the throne? He's still ordering your steps. That shaking is not going to defeat you; it's going to promote you. It is setting you up for what God is about to do. You're on the verge of something better than you've ever imagined. God is working behind the scenes. Things are in motion that you can't see. Thoughts will tell you, *It's not going to work out. You're not going to get well. Your child is never going to get back on course. This illness is going to ruin you financially.* No, the shaking is a sign that a shift is taking place. God is about to launch you to a new level. You're about to see something that you've never seen. It's not going to be ordinary. It's going to be uncommon, unusual, unprecedented favor, healing, opportunity. One day you'll look back and say, "Wow! What I thought was a bad break was really setting me up for this new level. The shaking wasn't there to stop me. The shaking is what shifted me into increase, into promotion, into talent that I hadn't known I had."

From Great Distress to Great Joy

Saul created so much havoc, so much opposition in Jerusalem, that the Scripture says, "Philip had to leave Jerusalem and go to Samaria." It doesn't say that Philip prayed and decided to go to Samaria. He didn't have a choice; he was forced out of Jerusalem. When you're doing the right thing and a door closes, somebody walks away, or the contract comes to an end that's not the enemy stopping you; that's God shifting you. The enemy may have meant it to harm you, but he doesn't have the final say. God wouldn't allow that door to close or that person to walk away if it were going to stop your purpose. Have a new perspective. It's shifting you to the new things that God has in store.

> You may get pushed out of Jerusalem, but Samaria is waiting for you.

I've learned that if you stay in faith when a door closes, God will open a bigger and a better door. You may get pushed out of Jerusalem, but Samaria is waiting for you. There's a place of victory, a place of abundance, that God has already prepared for you. There are people to whom God has already spoken about being good to you. There are people who will use their influence to push you forward. There are divine connections, people God has already ordained to come into your life. There are people who will love you, people who can't wait to be with you. Quit being discouraged over who pushed you out, who didn't want to be your friend, or who played politics and got the best of you. They didn't stop your destiny; they shifted you. They were a part of God's plan to push you forward. You're about to come into the new things God has in store.

> *Quit being discouraged over who pushed you out, who didn't want to be your friend, or who played politics and got the best of you. They didn't stop your destiny; they shifted you. They were a part of God's plan to push you forward.*

Philip arrived in Samaria, but it was not by choice. He was pushed out of Jerusalem. He could have been discouraged, but he understood this principle. He knew that God was still in control. What's interesting is that Samaria is where his ministry took off. Samaria is where he flourished and stepped into a new level. The Scripture says that Philip saw all kinds of miracles in Samaria. Blind eyes were opened, the crippled could walk, and great favor was on his life. He had never seen that in Jerusalem. If he would have stayed there, he would have missed the fullness of his destiny. Many times,

> *Many times, a great shaking precedes great favor. Great difficulty precedes great promotion. Great opposition precedes great influence.*

a great shaking precedes great favor. Great difficulty precedes great promotion. Great opposition precedes great influence.

If you could see what God is up to, you wouldn't be stressed over the shaking, complaining about the trouble, or upset over the setback. When you realize it's taking you to Samaria—a place where you're going to flourish, do things you've never dreamed, and see favor, abundance, and breakthroughs—you would thank

God even in the shakings. Even though it's uncertain, you would have a smile on your face and a spring in your step, knowing that God is up to something. All through the day you have to say, "Father, thank You that this shaking is not going to stop me, but it's going to shift me. It may have been meant for my harm, but I know it's leading me to my Samaria, where I'm going to flourish and see favor that I've never seen." Keep the right perspective. God never said there wouldn't be times when things are shaken, when things are unfair and we don't understand. That's not the time to fall apart. That's the time to kick your praise into a new gear. That's the time to speak victory over your life. That difficulty didn't come to stay; it came to pass. God being for you is more than the world being against you.

The Scripture says, "There was great joy in Samaria." Philip left Jerusalem in great distress. It was a great disappointment. But look at how God works. Philip went from great distress to great joy. He went from great trouble to great victory, from great rejection to people who loved him greatly. He didn't realize when he was having all the opposition in Jerusalem that great joy was waiting for him in Samaria. You may have gone through things that have caused you great pain, great disappointment, great loss. You could be bitter and live discouraged, but that is not how your story ends. As with Philip, great joy is coming, great favor, great relationships, great health. The enemy thought he was stopping you, but he didn't realize he was setting you up. In the shaking, God was shifting you.

> *He didn't realize when he was having all the opposition in Jerusalem that great joy was waiting for him in Samaria.*

You may not be there yet, but stay encouraged. You are headed toward great joy. It's not just joy, not just "I'm okay. I made it out.

Thank God that I'm still here." No, great joy is coming. Great victories are up ahead. You won't have to look back and think about the good old days and say, "I wish I was there." Can I tell you that there are some good new days in your future? The best days of your life are still in front of you. If you have gone through great disappointments, you need to declare every day, "Father, thank You that great joy is coming." The Scripture says, "God will fill your mouth with laughter." You're going to laugh again, you're going to love again, and you're going to dream again. Great joy is headed your way.

Getting You in a Position to Flourish

In 1999, my father had a heart attack and went to be with the Lord. I had worked with him for seventeen years behind the scenes at Lakewood. We were the best of friends. Outside of Victoria, I spent more time with my father than anyone else. I used to think, *What am I going to do when my father is gone?* When he suddenly died at seventy-seven years old, my whole world was turned upside down. I thought my father would live to be a hundred and fifty. He was my hero, but now he was gone. I've learned that in these times of shaking, God will always give us the grace that we need. The Scripture says, "God has armed us with strength for every battle." If we tap into that strength, we won't go around overwhelmed and stressed out. All these thoughts flooded my mind. *What's going to happen to the church? What if it doesn't make it? Who's going to be the pastor?* In the middle of all that turmoil, with so much uncertainty, I felt

> *In these times of shaking, God will always give us the grace that we need.*

a peace like I had never felt. It was something I can't explain. Even though I missed my father, I didn't get depressed or fall apart. I knew deep down that God was still in control.

What I didn't know at the time was that shaking was about to shift me. I never dreamed I would become a pastor. I never wanted to get up in front of people. But when my father suddenly passed, I had the desire to do it. I knew I was not only supposed to step up, but now I wanted to do it. My father had tried to get me up to minister for seventeen years, but I never had the desire. The psalmist says in Psalm 37, "God will give you the desires of your heart." Sometimes we think that means God will give us what we want. But another way to look at it is that God will put the desires in you. In that time of shaking, God shifted my desires. I didn't know if I would be any good as a pastor. I didn't know if people would keep coming. I was afraid and intimidated. But I thought, *I'm not going to come to the end of life and not know what might have happened if I had taken that step of faith.* Some opportunities don't pass by a second time. Out of that shaking, out of that loss, came talent that I hadn't known I had. Just as God pushed Philip out of Jerusalem and he began to flourish in Samaria, He had to push me out from behind the scenes to being in front of people.

It's significant that my flourishing, and Philip's flourishing, came out of a shaky time when there was uncertainty. When it looked as though nothing good was happening, God was, in fact, using that shaky season to shift us. He was getting us in position to flourish, to see His favor and blessings in new ways. In one sense, that's where we were in the pandemic. Things were shaking and uncertain. We'd never

> *When it looked as though nothing good was happening, God was, in fact, using that shaky season to shift us.*

seen this. There were so many questions: "When will life get back to normal? What about our finances? When can the children go back to school? How's it going to work out?" It's when you don't see anything positive, it's in the shaking that God is shifting you. It looks like a setback, but He's setting you up.

You're going to come into new opportunities. Doors that weren't open before are going to open for you. You're going to have desires that you've never had. Talent is going to come out that you hadn't known was in you. Because of this shift, where you've been told no before, you're going to hear yes. Yes to that business, yes to that new house, yes to that promotion, yes to that ministry. The shaking will change people's minds. Those who were not for you, who wouldn't give you the time of day, are going to be for you. Things have shifted. They're going to want to help you. During your medical checkup, you may have heard, "There's no improvement. No, nothing is getting better." Get ready for some yesses. Yes, you're getting healthier; yes, your blood pressure is back to normal; yes, the cancer is gone. There's some shifting taking place. You can't see it yet, but don't worry; you're coming into it. You don't have to find it; it's going to find you. It's already en route. The miracle is already in motion.

God is doing a new thing in your life. When your whole world seems like it's been put on pause, there are spiritual things happening. God is up to something big. He's looking for people like you whose hearts are turned toward Him. He's looking for people who honor Him, who keep Him first place. You're going to come out of this shaking into levels that you've never dreamed.

> When your whole world seems like it's been put on pause, there are spiritual things happening. God is up to something big.

Keep Him First Place

The writer of Proverbs says, "The wealth of the ungodly is laid up for the righteous." There are things God has laid up for you. There is going to be a transfer of wealth from people who have nothing to do with God, who only think about themselves, to people who will use the resources to build the kingdom, to lift the fallen, to feed the hungry, to bring justice to those who have no voice, to make the world a better place. God is about to shift some contracts, some businesses, some opportunities, some inheritances. It's going to be unusual income, things that you couldn't make happen. It's already headed your way. It's just a matter of time before you see God do unprecedented things. Now make sure that you keep Him first place. You don't have to seek the blessing; just seek Him and the blessings will seek you.

> *It's just a matter of time before you see God do unprecedented things.*

Part of the slowdown of the pandemic was an opportunity to draw closer to God. One thing the virus showed us is how little control we have. In spite of all the advances over the years—the airplane industry, the Internet, incredible technology, smart phones, heart transplants and other amazing medical procedures—this one coronavirus, this one seemingly small thing, shut down the whole world. If we put our trust in our finances, they can go down that quickly. If we put our trust in our job or our career, it can suddenly change. That's why it's so important to put your trust in God. He's the one who doesn't change. He's our source. That's where we get our strength, ideas, creativity, resources, and wisdom. God is the giver of all good things. Yes, we appreciate the companies where we work. We're grateful to have an income each week, but companies are not our source. They are simply a resource that the Source is using.

I believe the Source, the Most High God, is about to do some unusual, unprecedented things in your finances. You're going to lend and not borrow. He's going to prosper you even in a down-time. The Scripture says, "Even in a famine the righteous will have more than enough." Not just enough, but overflow. There are blessings that are going to come looking for you.

It's interesting that during the period in the pandemic when everything was closed down, we received a large payment to the ministry. It was something we had been owed for over ten years. It had to do with broadcast rights that I've had people explain to me three times, but I still don't understand. I've read about it, studied it, but I don't see how it applies to us. It doesn't make sense to me. But I stopped trying to figure it out, and I just received it. I believe it's one of those far-and-beyond blessings that God has laid up for the righteous. It's a part of the transfer of wealth. But it's interesting that it came at this uncertain time. The shaking is a sign that things are shifting in your favor. "Well, Joel, I don't believe that's going to happen for me." You're right; this is for believers. It's only going to happen if you release your faith and say, "Father, thank You that this shaking is shift-

> *It's only going to happen if you release your faith.*

ing me. Thank You that You're giving me new desires, giving me creativity, opening new doors. Thank You that You're blessing me so I can be a bigger blessing."

Your Samaria Is Already Lined Up

I talked to a lady who watches our television broadcast. She owns her own manufacturing business, has been very successful, and has stores that sell her product all over the country. A few years ago, things began to slow down. They made adjustments and were able to keep going, but they were struggling, barely surviving. One day she received word that thirty-six of her stores were closing. That was almost half of her business. She couldn't make it without that income. Her whole world was shaken. She had poured her heart and soul into that business, built it from the ground up. She never thought she would be in this position. All the circumstances said it was over. She could have accepted it and given up on her dream. But in the middle of that shaking, with all the uncertainty, she said, "God, I trust You. I know You're still in control. You can make a way where I don't see a way." A few weeks later, she got a call from a large company that she had never done business with before, saying they wanted to put her product in three hundred and sixty of their stores. Overnight she went from thirty-six stores to another three hundred and sixty. She thought she was going under, but suddenly she had ten times the amount of stores.

I've learned that God is not so much into addition; He's into multiplication. One touch of His favor will catapult you ahead. We look at our circumstances in the natural and think they could never work out, but we serve a supernatural God. He's not limited by what limits us. With one good break, one contract, or one phone call, God will multiply what you have. He'll thrust you to a new level. This lady would tell you that the shaking is a setup. It's a sign that God is about to shift things. There's going to be a shift in your finances, a shift in your career, a shift in your health, a shift in your marriage. It may be shaky right now, and things seem uncer-

> *God is not so much into addition; He's into multiplication.*

tain. You're tempted to live worried, to be stressed out. Get ready. A shift is coming. God is going to make things happen that you couldn't make happen.

Perhaps your medical report doesn't look good. It's shaking your world. Come back to a place of peace. God can do what medicine cannot do. He promised that the number of your days, He will fulfill. Maybe your child is off course, your business went down, or you're in a legal situation. You never dreamed you would be dealing with this. It's keeping you awake at night. But it's not a surprise to God. He wouldn't allow the shaking if He didn't already have a solution. If He didn't have Samaria already lined up, He wouldn't allow the trouble in Jerusalem. Instead of being stressed over the shaking, why don't you start thanking Him for the solution? "Father, thank You that a shift is coming, breakthroughs, healing, favor. Thank You that what You started in my life, You will finish."

> *Instead of being stressed over the shaking, why don't you start thanking Him for the solution?*

You Will Fulfill Your Purpose

In Acts 16, the apostle Paul and Silas had been put in prison for sharing their faith. They were in the deepest dungeon, with chains around their feet. The authorities were so afraid of their influence that they went to great lengths to make sure they couldn't escape. But God will never let you get in a problem that He can't get you out of. It may look as though your situation doesn't have a solution. The odds are against you. But God has ways of doing things you've never thought of. What's impossible with people is possible with God. At midnight, Paul and Silas were singing praises and thanking God. The Scripture says, "Suddenly there came a great earthquake. All the foundations of the prison were shaken, immediately the doors were opened, and everyone's chains were unfastened." Notice what the shaking did. It opened prison doors. It unloosed chains that were restricting them. Paul and Silas walked out as free men.

The shaking on the surface may have seemed like a negative thing, but without the shaking Paul wouldn't have fulfilled his purpose. The shaking was necessary for Paul to become who he was created to be. We may not like the shakings, the times when things seem out of control, but as with Paul, they're not going to stop you; they're going to shift you. Out of this shaking, new doors are going to open, new opportunities, new relationships. Things that you didn't see are coming. Chains that have held you back are about to be unfastened—chains of depression, chains of lack and struggle, chains of addictions. Don't complain about the shaking. It's serving a purpose. God is using it to thrust you where you couldn't go without it.

> *The shaking was necessary for Paul to become who he was created to be.*

Now every day you have to say, "Father, thank You that this shaking is shifting me into promotion, into healing, into new levels." If you keep this attitude of faith as Philip did, I believe and declare that you're going to come out of the shaking into great joy, great favor, great increase, and great relationships.

CHAPTER SIX

Something New Is Coming

It's easy to get stuck in life. When we've gone through disappointments, had a setback, tried hard but our dream didn't work out, we can settle where we are and think this is as good as it gets. But God says in Isaiah 43, "See, I am doing a new thing. Even now it springs forth. Can you not perceive it?" God is about to do something new in your life. He didn't create you to get stuck at one level and stay there. He has new opportunities, new relationships, new favor. It may look as though you'll always struggle in your finances. No, get ready. Something new is coming—promotion, opportunities, doors opening that you never dreamed would open.

Maybe the medical report says you have to live with the sickness that you've had for a long time. God is saying, "I'm doing a new thing. I'm restoring health. I'm breathing energy, vitality, freshness into your body." Perhaps your child has been off course for years, and you've accepted that he'll never change. That would be true, but God is doing a new thing. Forces of darkness are being broken. Purpose and destiny are rising up in his life. You're about to see a turnaround. Maybe you've had an addiction that has hindered you for most of your life. You've tried to stop, gone to counseling, but nothing has helped. This is a new day. Chains that have held you back are being loosed. What's kept you in captivity is coming to an end. Now you have to do your part and receive the prophecy. You can't go around thinking that you're stuck, that the problem is too big, that it's been this way too long. Turn it around. "Lord, I believe what You promised. Thank You that You're doing a new thing in my life."

When Isaiah prophesied this, the Israelites had been in captivity in Babylon for a long time. Year after year, nothing was changing. I'm sure they thought, *We'll always struggle. We'll always be oppressed.* Then Isaiah showed up and said, "Get ready. God says He is doing a new thing." They could have thought, *Yeah, right. Have you seen these enemies? Look how powerful they are. All the circumstances say we're stuck. We'll never live an abundant life. We'll never own our own homes, and our children will never be free.* Don't talk yourself out of the new thing God wants to do. The odds may be against you, but the Most High God is for you.

> *Don't talk yourself out of the new thing God wants to do.*

Forget the Former Things

The Israelites had been through many struggles and had unfair things happen to them. They had made mistakes and brought the trouble on themselves. They could have been discouraged, sitting in self-pity. But Isaiah said, "Forget the former things. Do not dwell on the past. Behold, God is doing a new thing." The principle is: If you're dwelling on the past, you won't see the new thing.

If you're focused on who hurt you and what wasn't fair, on why a friend walked away, you'll miss your destiny. God is saying, "Forget the former things. Quit dwelling on your mistakes. This is a new day." Living in regrets will keep you from new opportunities, and reliving your mistakes will stop the new favor. As long as you're looking back at the old, you won't see the new. When you drive your car,

> *Is there something you need to forget so you can see the new thing?*

there's a big windshield in front of you and a very small rearview mirror. The reason the mirror is so small is because what's behind you is not nearly as important as what's in front of you. Where you're going is what matters, not where you've been. Is there something you need to forget so you can see the new thing? Is there something you need to quit dwelling upon so you can step into the favor and abundance that God has for you?

When someone hurts you, when they do you wrong, if you keep thinking about it, you're letting them continue to hurt you. Don't give them your power. You have to let it go. Give it to God. He saw what they did. He saw your tears, your heartache. He has beauty for those ashes. But here's the key: You have to let go of the ashes before you can see the beauty. It's an exchange. God says, "You give me the ashes, you quit dwelling on the hurts, you forgive them, you move forward with your life, and I'll give you the beauty. I'll do something so great, so rewarding, that you won't even think about what you've lost." The new thing God has for you—the new people, the new opportunities, the promotion, healing, influence—will be better than you ever dreamed.

The Israelites were in captivity. Not only were the Babylonians holding them there, but all around them was the desert. Even if they escaped, they couldn't survive the journey home. But Isaiah explained what the new thing was. He said, "God will make rivers in the desert. What looks like barren ground will be turned into fertile land." God was saying, "This new thing I'm about to do is not going to be natural; it's going to be supernatural." That's why you can't figure it out. It's not going to be logical. What God is about to do is going to be unusual, uncommon, out of the ordinary. You're going to see rivers where there should be dry places. Remember that He says, "Even in famine the righteous will have more than enough." It seems as though in a famine you would barely get by. But God does things that defy the odds. Don't limit this new thing to what you think can happen. "If I can just learn to live with this sickness." No, God is going to free you from the sickness.

> *Don't limit this new thing to what you think can happen.*

"If I can just pay my bills, I'll be happy." God is going to bring you into overflow. "If my child will just stay out of trouble." That child is going to do great things. You may not see how. That's okay. It's not up to you. It's up to God. He's the one who makes rivers in the desert. He's the one who parts Red Seas, cures the lepers, and multiplies the food to feed thousands.

Rivers in the Desert

A lady told me how her relative had passed away and left her a small inheritance that she decided to invest in real estate. She bought a second house and rented it out. The first couple who answered her ad seemed like fine people. They worked for a nonprofit that helped children. Because she thought they would be perfect, she didn't do all the background checks that she should have. It turned out that they were dishonest. Three months into the lease they stopped paying rent and didn't tell her. She had the account set up for their payments to go to the bank, and she thought everything was fine. But the couple found a way to keep her from getting the bank notices. Several years went by, and eventually the house was foreclosed on, and she lost all her money. She could have been upset, gotten bitter, and tried to get revenge. But she said, "I didn't make a big deal about it." That takes maturity. It's easy to make a big deal when we're hurt and betrayed. "Why did this happen? I'm going to get even." You have to forget the former things. Do not dwell on the past. That means you don't let the hurts, the bad breaks, or the times you were taken advantage of sour the rest of your life and cause you to live with a chip on your shoulder. God knows how to vindicate you. He knows how to pay you back.

Year after year this lady kept being her best. Nobody even knew she had gone through the bad break. She didn't go around complaining, being discouraged. She had a song of praise. God sees when you're in the desert. He's watching you in the lonely nights, the times when you were betrayed, when you felt like giving up but you kept going. You could have held a grudge, but you forgave. You kept moving forward. It wasn't easy. You were hurting, and the pain was real,

> *This new thing He's going to do will be supernatural.*

but you didn't let it stop you. Six years later, this lady got an unexpected check in the mail from the bank for $125,000. They said, "We sold the property, and this money belongs to you." She hadn't even paid that much for it. She made a profit. God knows how to make rivers in the desert. He knows how to pay you back for the wrongs. This new thing He's going to do will be supernatural.

He's going to turn barren ground into fertile ground. What looks like a loss is going to turn into a gain. It seems like a setback, but it's really a setup for God to show out in your life.

The desert represents barrenness, no growth. You're doing the right thing, but your business is not increasing, your marriage is not getting better, your health is not improving, or you're passed over for another promotion. You're in the desert. In those dry places, you could be discouraged and think it will never change. No, get ready. God is about to make rivers in that desert. He's about to turn that barren land into fertile ground. As with this lady, you're going to see increase that you can't explain, favor that you don't deserve, healing that doesn't make sense, freedom from things that have held you back.

Now It Springs Forth

When Isaiah prophesied this, the people could have said, "Thanks, Isaiah, but we've had too many bad breaks. The opposition is too big. We'll never get out." You can stop the prophecy from coming to pass. The psalmist says, "They limited the Holy One of Israel." You can limit what God wants to do in your life by doubt, negativity, speaking defeat. "My business is never going to grow. I'll never meet the right person. I haven't had a date in years. Have you seen all that I've been through?" You are canceling out the prophecy. You may have obstacles that look too big. You don't see how you can accomplish that dream. It feels as though you're stuck, you're in captivity, restricted by your environment. God is saying to you what He said to them: "I am doing a new thing. I'm making rivers in that desert. I'm turning the barren places into fertile ground." Now get in agreement with God and say, "Yes, Lord, this is for me today. I receive it into my spirit. I'm getting ready for something new. Lord, amaze me with Your goodness. Turn this problem around. God, show out in my life."

It's significant that this promise is in the present tense. God didn't say, "I'm about to do a new thing. One day I'm going to work in your life. Sometime in the future I'm going to show you My goodness." God says, "I am doing a new thing." It's already started. What God has for you is already set in motion. This new thing is already in process. The Scripture says, "Now it springs forth." To "spring forth" refers to when a seed is planted in the ground. You can't see anything happening, but the seed has opened up. It's springing forth even though it may not become visible for some time. There are promotions, healings, breakthroughs, and divine connections that have already sprung forth. It's already en route. Just because you don't see it doesn't mean it's not coming. This is where your faith has to kick in. There should be an expectancy and not a looking back that says, "This downturn is so hard. My back's been hurting. My company did me wrong. I'm in the desert, Joel. That's why I'm discouraged."

> God says, "I am doing a new thing." It's already started.

As long as you're looking back, you're going to miss the new thing. You have to get prepared in your thinking. *By faith, I can see the healing that's coming. I can see promotion on its way. I can see my child turning around. I can see myself free from this addiction.* Now it springs forth—not one day, not in the sweet by-and-by. Today, God is doing a new thing. Today, God is making rivers in your desert. Today, God is turning your dry places into abundant places. If you stay in

> As long as you're looking back, you're going to miss the new thing.

faith, you're going to see the new thing. As God did for the Israelites, He's going to bring you out of captivity. He's going to free you
from limitations and negative things that have been passed down
in your family line. In this new thing, God is going to break gen-
erational curses, addictions, poverty, and depression will no longer
hold you back. There's about to be streams in that desert. That
barren land is about to be turned into fertile land, an abundant
land, with dreams coming to pass. He's going to catapult you to
where no one in your family has gone.

Can You Not Perceive It?

I talked to a single mom named Sherree who lives and teaches
school in Compton, California. There are a lot of great people in
Compton, but the city is known for having a rough environment,
with gangs and drugs. Her husband was in the federal penitentiary, so for thirteen years she raised her son, EJayy, by herself.
As a child, he would sometimes lie on the floor as gunshots were
fired right outside his bedroom window. There were a lot of negative influences and opportunities for him to get off course, but
she's a praying mother. Even though she was in a dry place, she
knew that God could make streams in the desert. It seemed as
though they were held captive by their environment, victims of
their circumstances. Her son could have become another statistic,
another child struggling, off course, on drugs. But she believed
God was doing a new thing, that He was working behind the
scenes. Every morning before they went to school, they would
listen to our messages, starting the day off in faith and hope and
victory.

This mother's dream was for her son to go to college. All the odds were against him. Sherree didn't have the funds. His father was in prison. During his senior year, EJayy applied to several different colleges and was waiting to hear back. One morning on their way to school, they heard me talking about how God has unprecedented favor, how He can make things happen that we can't make happen, how He wants to do a new thing. Sherree heard that promise and something came alive inside. She told EJayy, "That's for us." Later that day, he received a handwritten letter in the mail that said, "Congratulations, you've been accepted into Harvard University." His story made national news, and when we met with his mother, she told us that he was the first African American student from Compton ever accepted into Harvard.

God knows how to make rivers in the desert. He knows how to bring you out of the captivity of struggle, lack, addictions, depression, can't get a good break. Get ready. Your time is coming. God is doing a new thing. You may be in a dry place, but you're not going to stay there. Water is coming. Favor, promotion, healing, and freedom are coming. Get your hopes up. Start expecting God's favor. Start believing for the unusual. God wants to make you an example of His goodness. He's already set in motion something better than you can imagine. You can't see it yet, but that doesn't mean it's not en route. Keep believing, keep talking like it's on the way, keep doing the right thing. As with the Israelites, you're going to see God exceed your expectations.

> *He knows how to bring you out of the captivity of struggle, lack, addictions, depression, can't get a good break.*

EJayy became a member of the 2021 graduating class at

Harvard, was chosen as a Rhodes Scholar, one of only thirty-two from America, and is studying in England at Oxford University. He has also been accepted to Yale Law School. If you could see what God is doing behind the scenes in your life, you would be amazed. He's already lined up the good breaks, the right people, solutions to problems. The new thing is not going to be ordinary. It's going to catapult you ahead. You're not going to stay in any kind of captivity. Don't believe the lies that say you're stuck. "Look at my environment. Look at how I was raised. I don't have the funds for my dreams. I'll always be restricted by these limitations." That's what it looked like for this young man, and that's how it looked for the Israelites in Babylon. But God showed up and said, "I'm doing a new thing. I'm going to make rivers in the desert." God is saying that to you. Where you are is not your destiny. You haven't reached your limits. You haven't seen your best days. This new thing is going to be something that you've never seen.

> *This new thing is going to be something that you've never seen.*

The Scripture says, "Can you not perceive it?" It implies that God can be doing it, but there's no sign of it. "Joel, I don't see anything new happening in my life. I'm still struggling, still lonely, still sick. I still have this problem at work." Yes, but what you can't see is the new thing has already sprung forth. It's already in motion. This mother could have thought that nothing was happening for many years. When EJayy was thirteen, she didn't have the funds for college. When he was fourteen, still no funds; at fifteen, nothing better. She was in the desert, with no sign of rivers. There was no sign that things were going to change. But just because you don't see anything doesn't mean it's not on the way. At the right time, it's going to show up. You could see your new thing tomorrow. You could see your breakthrough this week. You could get that scholarship this month. You could see your healing, your promotion, or your abundance this year.

It's a New Thing, Not an Old Thing

When God says He's going to do a new thing, that means it's not going to be like the old thing. It's going to be different. The new thing may not be what you were expecting. It may not happen the way you thought it would. The Israelites could have thought, *God, just defeat these Babylonians and we'll live here.* They didn't think that God would take them into the desert.

> *Stay open for how God is going to do it. Don't put Him in a box and limit Him to one way.*

How could they survive out there? God was going to do it a different way. He was going to make streams in the desert. Stay open for how God is going to do it. Don't put Him in a box and limit Him to one way. Most of the time, the way we want it done is less than what God has in mind. What He has planned will be much bigger, much better. Trust Him to do it His way. If we're set in how we want it to happen, we can miss the new thing.

Victoria and I were in another city driving a rental car recently. She ran into a store to shop for what she said would be about fifteen minutes. I waited in the car and started making some calls. After an hour, my phone battery died. I usually bring my phone charger to plug into the car, but I forgot it. I looked in the glove compartment for one, then looked in Victoria's bag, but nothing. I sat there and waited and waited, thinking about all the work I could be doing. At one point, I looked down by the gear shift and saw a rubber pad, about the size of a phone. I thought that

> *Can I tell you that some of the new things God is going to do in your life are not going to be what you're expecting?*

was interesting, and I sat my phone on it. I heard my phone buzz, and it started charging. Here I had a charger the whole time, but it wasn't what I was used to. I thought there would be a cord and I would have to plug it in. Can I tell you that some of the new things God is going to do in your life are not going to be what you're expecting? He's going to do it a different way, with different people, in different circumstances. Could it be that God is doing a new thing now and you don't perceive it? He's opening a door, but you don't want to go through it because it's not what you thought it would look like. He's bringing people across your path who are divine connections, but they're not who you were expecting. Don't get set in your ways. The new thing may not look like what you had in mind.

A few years after I started ministering at Lakewood, the church began to grow. I thought we would build a new auditorium, which is the way I had seen my father do it when I was growing up. He had built sanctuary after sanctuary. Close to our old location, we found some property right off the freeway that seemed perfect to me, but when we went to close on it, the owner sold it out from under us. He didn't keep his word. I was disappointed. I knew that property was supposed to be ours. Then we found another hundred-acre tract of land not far away, and the same thing happened. I couldn't understand why the doors kept closing. There were no more large tracts of land to build on by our old location. My father had always said that he would never move the church. My mind wasn't open for the new thing God had in store. About six months later, the Compaq Center came available. I never dreamed we could have this building. This was so much bigger and better than I ever imagined. It was a three-year battle, but we saw the hand of God make rivers in the desert, move giants out of the way, and bring the right people to help us.

We had a consultant who was very influential and knew all the inner workings of the city. He had never been to church and didn't have anything to do with God or faith. He partied, used bad language, and was known to curse people out. But he said, "Joel, I like you, and I'm going to help you get this building." God has already lined up the people you need for the new thing. Stay open. It may not happen the way you're expecting, but God's way will be better, bigger, more rewarding, and more fulfilling. Don't limit what you've seen in the past to what God is going to do in your future. God never does His greatest feats in your yesterdays; they are always in your tomorrows.

> *God has already lined up the people you need for the new thing.*

Be Prepared to Say "Wow!"

God says in Isaiah, "I am the one who opened a way through the waters, making a dry path through the sea. I called forth the mighty armies of Pharaoh and drowned them in the waters. But forget about all of that. It's nothing compared to what I'm about to do, for I am doing a brand-new thing." This brand-new thing is not going to be like anything you've seen in the past. We all can look back and see where God has parted Red Seas in our lives. We've seen Him open a door that shouldn't have opened and had us in the right place at the right time. We got the job. We met the right person and fell in love. God turned our health around when it didn't look good. We're grateful. We know it was the hand of God. But God is saying, "You haven't seen anything yet. Forget about all that and get ready for something awesome, something that you haven't seen, something that propels you to a new level." When you see this new thing, you're going to stand in amazement and say, "Wow, look what the Lord has done!"

I believe the reason God told them to forget about the Red Sea being parted and forget about how He brought them out of slavery is because they would have thought He was going to do it the same way. After all, that was a great miracle. But God was saying, "I have something better. Instead of parting the waters, I'm going to create the waters. I'm going to make rivers in the desert, pools to refresh you. I'm going to turn barren land into fertile land." The new thing God has for you is going to supersede what you've seen in the past. The good news is that it's already in motion, the process has already begun. Even now it's springing forth. Underground, behind the scenes, you can't see it, but the river is forming, the water is coming, and the barren land is being fertilized. Yes, the doors may have closed, but don't worry. Your Compaq Center is already built. The right people are already en route. The Red Sea parting was great, but it's nothing compared to what's coming.

> *Do you believe that God is up to something amazing, or are you looking back at what used to be, at what didn't work out?*

Here's the question: Can you perceive it? Do you believe that God is up to something amazing, or are you looking back at what used to be, at what didn't work out? Change your focus. No more looking in the rearview mirror. Start looking forward, start expecting His goodness.

This is a new day. God is doing a new thing in your life. If you receive Isaiah's prophecy in your spirit, I believe and declare you're about to see unusual favor, uncommon increase. You will see rivers in your desert, water in the dry places. Like the Israelites, you'll have freedom from captivity, from lack, addictions, sicknesses. You're going to rise higher, overcome obstacles, and become all you were created to be.

CHAPTER SEVEN

It's Coming Together

When we've struggled in an area for a long time, it easy to think it's never going to work out. Our dream is too big, the medical report is too negative, or our family is so dysfunctional that we don't see how we could ever be restored. As the months go by, sometimes even years, and we don't see anything happening, it's easy to get discouraged and give up on what we're believing for. But just because you don't see anything happening doesn't mean that God is not working. Behind the scenes He's arranging things in your favor, lining up the right people, the healing, the promotion, the favor. If you stay in faith, at the right time you will see it come together. What you couldn't make happen on your own, God will make happen for you. Your dream is coming together. Your relationship is coming together. The healing, the promotion, and the vindication will all come together.

A friend of mine had been in a legal battle over a business dispute for six years. Some people had made false accusations against him, trying to take his company. He knew he was in the right. He thought the dispute would take three or four months to clear up, but it dragged on year after year. He's had to fight the thoughts telling him, *This is going to make you look bad and ruin your career.*

It's never going to work out. It's going to bankrupt your business. He could have been discouraged and bitter. Instead, all through the day he would say, "Lord, thank You that You're my vindicator. Thank You that You're fighting my battles." He was saying, in effect, "Thank You that it's coming together." One day, unexpect-edly, the other side called the judge and admitted that they had made up the accusations, that it was totally false. The case was dismissed. Suddenly it all came together. He was vindicated. It may not happen on your timetable, but I can assure you that God is a faithful God. He says in Hebrews 13, "I will not, I will not, I will not in any way fail you." God said it three times because He knew how easy it is for us to give up on our dreams, to let our circumstances and how long it's been talk us out of His best.

> *"I will not, I will not, I will not in any way fail you."*

You may have a situation that looks impossible today. You've had some setbacks, and the odds are against you. Let me encourage you that it's coming together. God is not going to fail you. The breakthrough is already in your future. That person you've been dreaming about, you're not going to have to find them; they're going to find you. Your relationship is coming together. Don't believe the lie that you'll have to live your life lonely. The right person has already been ordained to cross your path. Or you may think you can never get out of debt, never live in a nice house, never be successful in your career. You may think you've gone as far as your education allows. No, don't talk yourself out of it. It's coming together. Promotion, abundance, and new levels are headed your way.

When you go through the day with this expectancy, knowing that God is working behind the scenes and bringing it together, that's what allows God to do great things. You could be complaining, but instead you're saying, "Lord, thank You that my healing is coming together. You can do what medicine cannot do. Or that business, that dream, that orphanage You've put in my heart. Lord, thank You that the connections, the funding, and the permits are all coming together."

> *When you go through the day with this expectancy, knowing that God is working behind the scenes and bringing it together, that's what allows God to do great things.*

Prophesy to What Looks Dead

In the Scripture, the prophet Ezekiel saw a vision of a valley filled with dry bones. It was a huge graveyard with thousands and thousands of bones on the ground. God told Ezekiel to speak to the bones and they would come back to life. He could have thought, *That's impossible. They're just disjointed, dried-up bones. They can't live. It's too late.* But in this vision he started prophesying to the dead bones. The Scripture says, "There was a noise, a rattling sound, and the bones came together, bone to bone." All at once these bones joined back into the right places with tendons. Then the organs came, the body tissues, the flesh. Then God breathed life into them, and they stood up like a vast army.

The Israelites had been discouraged, living in captivity. They were saying, "Our bones are dried up. Our hope is gone. We've been cut off." In other words, they were saying, "We're just slaves. We're never going to reach our destiny. We're just dead, dry bones." God said, "Ezekiel, go tell My people the Sovereign Lord says, 'I'm about to open up your graves. I'm going to take you back to your land, and you will know that I am the Lord.'" He was saying,

"Ezekiel, go tell them what you saw in this vision, that there's about to be a great coming together. What they couldn't make happen on their own, I'm going to supernaturally make happen for them."

On your own, your situation may be impossible. The good news is that you're not on your own. You have the most powerful force in the universe on your side. One touch of God's favor can catapult you to a new level. But as with the Israelites, what you have may seem dead. The medical report says you'll never get well. You lost a loved one, and you don't see how you can ever be happy again. You've been through some bad breaks. Now all you have are dead bones, disjointed and broken pieces. There is no way in the natural to put it back together. But the Sovereign Lord is saying to you what He said to the Israelites: "Get ready. There's about to be a great coming together." God is going to bring things to life that you thought were dead. Maybe you have a dream you've given up on, but suddenly the right people show up, suddenly you get the break you need, suddenly the funding comes through. Perhaps you've been strug-

> *God is going to bring things to life that you thought were dead.*

gling with an illness for years, and you don't think you can ever get well. No, get ready. Health is about to spring forth. God knows how to bring the pieces back together. By faith I can hear a noise, a rattling sound. It's the sound of a great coming together. I can hear the sound of abundance, the sound of healing, the sound of promotion, the sound of victory.

At the first part of this vision, God asked Ezekiel, "Can these dead bones live?" Ezekiel could have looked at it in the natural and thought, *No way. That's impossible.* Instead he looked away from the circumstances and looked toward his God. He said, "Sovereign Lord, You alone know." He was saying, "God, You control the universe. You have the final say. You're the giver of life. You part Red

Seas. You open blind eyes. You stopped the sun for Joshua. I may not see a way, but Sovereign Lord, I know You have a way." God said, in effect, "All right, Ezekiel, that's what I'm looking for. I'm not looking for a doubter, a complainer, or somebody who's going to tell Me all the reasons why it's not going to happen. I'm looking for someone like you, someone who's full of faith. I'm looking for people who know all things are possible." God told Ezekiel to prophesy to those dead bones.

> *If you have a poor mouth, you're going to have a poor life.*

Whatever looks dead in your life, you need to prophesy victory, prophesy wholeness, prophesy abundance. You may be struggling in your finances. Don't go around talking about how you'll never get ahead, how prices are too high, how you can't afford what you need. If you have a poor mouth, you're going to have a poor life. Dare to prophesy the promise from Deuteronomy 28, "I am the head and not the tail. Whatever I touch will prosper and succeed." Maybe you're up against a big obstacle. Don't talk about how big your problem is; talk about how big your God is. Dare to prophesy to that sickness, "Cancer, you can't defeat me. I'm a child of the Most High God." If your son is off course, don't call your friends and talk about how bad he is, how he's going to give you a nervous breakdown, how he keeps running with the wrong crowd. No, prophesy, "My son will fulfill his destiny. I am calling out his seeds of greatness. No weapon formed against my family will ever prosper." When you get in agreement with God, when you speak life

> *When you get in agreement with God, when you speak life and faith and favor and health, you're going to see a great coming together.*

and faith and favor and health, you're going to see a great coming together. Suddenly you'll get the break you need. Suddenly your business will turn around. Suddenly your health will improve. God will do what you couldn't do.

Keep On Prophesying

My father wasn't raised with any spiritual upbringing. His parents and family were fine people, cotton farmers, but they didn't know anything about God. At the age of seventeen, my dad gave his life to Christ, the first one in the family. Against all odds, he left the farm and went on to become a successful pastor. Over the years he would go home and talk to his family about the Lord. His mother and some other relatives were open and put their faith in Christ. But his father wouldn't have anything to do with God. He said, "John, I don't need any of that religious stuff. That's not for me. When I'm dead, I'll be dead like a dog. Just roll me over in a ditch." My dad would tell him, "No, Dad, you have to live on somewhere," but it went in one ear and out the other. This went on year after year. It looked as though those dead, dry bones would never change. But my father didn't get discouraged or start complaining. He kept prophesying to those dead bones. He kept saying, "Father, You say, 'As for me and my house we will serve the Lord.' " All through the day, instead of worrying, he would say, "Lord, thank You that You're working behind the scenes. I believe these dead bones can live. I believe You will reveal Yourself to my father."

One Sunday, my dad was a guest minister in the town where his parents lived. He had been talking to his father for thirty years with no response. My dad was standing in the podium giving his message when he saw his father walk into the church and sit down in the back row. This was the first time his dad had ever been in church. My father was thrilled. As my dad continued his message, his father got up and walked down the center aisle toward the platform. He didn't stop at the altar, and he didn't stop at the stairs. He came all the way up on the platform, stood right next to my father, and interrupted his sermon. He said, "John, I'm finishing today what I started over thirty years ago. I want to give my life to Christ." My father prayed with him right there in front of the whole congregation. It was a dream come true.

Afterward, my dad asked him what he meant about finishing what he started years earlier. His father told him how one day he was out in the woods when he got caught in a huge snowstorm. He couldn't see anything and lost his sense of direction. Night came, and he was lost. He was certain that he was going to freeze to death that night, so he had prayed for the first time and said, "God, if You will let me live, I will serve You." He fell asleep there in the snow, knowing that his body was shutting down. But he woke up the next morning as warm as toast. God had spared his life. All those years he'd been putting it off. He said, "Today, I'm keeping my promise. I'm going to do what I told God I would do."

> *He fell asleep there in the snow, knowing that his body was shutting down. But he woke up the next morning as warm as toast. God had spared his life.*

He gave his life to Christ, joined that church, and not long after that they asked him to become an usher. He was so proud that you would have thought they'd asked him to become the president of the United States. He never missed a service. He was very poor and only owned one suit, but he wore that same suit to every service. Years later when he died, he was buried in that suit. At the funeral, they found gospel tracts stuffed in his front pockets that he would pass out everywhere he went.

God knows how to bring it all together. What you think is dead, over, too far gone, you better get ready. It's coming together. People who you think will never change, such as my grandfather, God has already planted seeds in their heart. God has been working behind the scenes in your life since the day you were born, arranging the breaks you need, moving the wrong people out of the way, lining up the favor and advantages. He's got it all figured out. You don't have to worry. God has you in the palms of His hands. He's not going to fail you. He is faithful to His promises. Your family is coming together. The dream may look too big, but keep believing that it's coming together. God has a way. Don't give up on the addiction you've been trying to break for years. Keep prophesying. Freedom is coming together.

> God knows how to bring it all together.

He's Getting You Prepared

When you realize that God is in control, that He's directing your steps, that He's already lined up everything you need, then you can relax. You don't have to go through life trying to make it all happen on your own. You don't have to live worried about your children, or frustrated because the promotion is taking too long, or discouraged because a dream looks dead. No, keep reminding yourself: The Sovereign Lord is the God who breathed life into you, the God who knew you before you were born, the God who has planned out your days for good, and the God who has protected you, promoted you, and healed you. The same God who brought you to where you are is going to get you to where you're supposed to be. It may take a little longer than you thought, but that's okay. God's timing is the perfect time. It may not happen the way you had planned. My father never thought his dad would interrupt him in the pulpit,

> *The same God who brought you to where you are is going to get you to where you're supposed to be.*

but God's ways are not our ways. They are better than our ways. It's coming together.

When my father went to be with the Lord in 1999, I knew I was supposed to step up to pastor the church. I felt it so strongly, but I didn't know if I could do it. I liked being where I was, behind the scenes. I had spent the previous seventeen years doing the production at the church and editing my father's sermons. But I took that step of faith, not knowing what was going to happen. Looking back now, I can see how God was guiding me all that time. When I edited my father's sermons, I had to listen to the messages five or six times in order to cut them down to time. All those years, all those Scriptures, all those stories were going into me over and over, getting me prepared for what I'm doing now. I never dreamed I would become a minister, but it all came together. What I needed, God had already put in me. I never dreamed we'd have church

in the former Compaq Center, but it all came together. It has been way more than we could ask or think of.

Are you worrying about your future? Are you worried about how you're going to accomplish a dream, how you're going to raise your children, or how you're ever going to meet the right person? God has

> *You may not even realize how God is getting you prepared right now for something much greater, much bigger, than you've ever dreamed.*

already lined it up. He's already arranged everything you need. As with me, you may not even realize how God is getting you prepared right now for something much greater, much bigger, than you've ever dreamed. Keep honoring Him, keep being your best, keep prophesying life to those dead areas. You are going to see it all come together and be more than you imagined.

Stay in Peace

Our daughter, Alexandra, was two months old when my father died. Jonathan was three. Our lives suddenly changed. Taking over the pastoring of a large church, Victoria and I had a lot more responsibility. Plus, having never ministered before made it even more stressful. We knew we had to find some help with our children. We wanted to find the perfect person, someone very loving and kind who would treat them the way we did. We really didn't know where to start to look. One Sunday, Victoria was walking by the front platform when she saw a young man she'd seen there many times. He seemed very nice and wholesome, always faithful. Victoria went over and struck up a conversation, eventually asking him what his mother did for a living. He said, "She doesn't have a full-time job. She does a lot of volunteer work." Victoria told him that we were looking for someone to care for our children. We ended up meeting with her, and things fell into place. She was a perfect fit. Our children loved her like our own family. She was always laughing, loving, easygoing. We couldn't have found a better person.

What's interesting is that about a year after this lady started working for us, she told us that years earlier she had had a dream in which she was taking care of a beautiful, blue-eyed, blond-haired baby girl. This woman is Hispanic, has two sons of her own, and didn't understand what the dream meant. But when she saw little Alexandra, with the blond hair and blue eyes, she said, "She's the baby that I saw in my dream." What am I saying? God has the right people already lined up for you. At the right time it's all going to come together. You don't have to worry. You don't have to live stressed out. God is directing your steps. He controls the whole universe. You can stay in a place of peace.

> *God has the right people already lined up for you. At the right time it's all going to come together.*

In the Scripture, after a lady named Ruth lost her husband, she had to go into the harvest fields and pick up any leftover grain the workers missed. She was just trying to survive, barely making it. Boaz, the owner of the fields, spoke to his workers about Ruth, telling them to leave wheat on the ground on purpose for her, making it easier for her. He didn't speak to Ruth; he spoke about Ruth. She never heard what he said, but her life suddenly got a whole lot easier. She had more wheat than she needed. Her work in the field was finished in half the time. All because somebody she didn't even know put in a good word for her. In the same way, God has already spoken to the right people to be good to you, to bless you, to show you favor, to open the right doors. As with Ruth, suddenly you will come into blessings that you didn't work for. People will go out of their way to help you succeed. You may never know why it happened. That's God working behind the scenes, bringing it all together.

A Great Coming Together

In Chapter Four, I described the story of how God had put a dream in Moses' heart that he would deliver the people of Israel out of slavery, but he got in a hurry and didn't wait for God's timing. Because he killed an Egyptian foreman who was mistreating a Hebrew slave, he had to flee for his life and spent the next forty years hiding in the backside of the desert. It looked as though he'd missed his destiny. I'm sure he felt like a failure. Thoughts told him, *Too bad, Moses. You had your chance. That mistake really did you in.* Moses had been raised in the palace of one of Pharaoh's daughters. He was trained to be a prince, educated by the best scholars, and spoke different languages. He was gifted, talented, and had been prepared to do something great. But instead of wearing his royal robe, he wore dirty old, smelly shepherd's clothes. Instead of conducting his business in the palace where he was esteemed and respected, he spent his days taking care of sheep, shoveling their waste out in the middle of the desert.

Year after year went by. Moses must have thought, *I heard God wrong. Maybe I was never supposed to deliver the people of Israel. Maybe I'm not supposed to do something great. What was I thinking?* Just when Moses was about to give up, suddenly a bush in the wilderness exploded into flames right in front of him. When he went over to get a better look at it, he heard a voice saying, "Moses! Take off your sandals. You are standing on holy ground." God was saying, "Moses, I haven't forgotten about you. You made some mistakes and took some wrong turns, but get ready. I'm about to bring it together. What I promised you, I'm still going to bring to pass." After forty years of not seeing anything happening, suddenly God turned it around. Moses went out and delivered the people of Israel.

> *Just when Moses was about to give up, suddenly a bush in the wilderness exploded into flames right in front of him.*

You may think, *Joel, it could never come together for me. It's been too long. I've made too many mistakes. I've missed too many opportunities.* In your heart you know what God has promised you, but in your mind the enemy will whisper these thoughts of doubt. *Maybe I'm not supposed to get married. Maybe I'm not supposed to break this addiction. Maybe I'm not supposed to start my own business.* Deep down you feel seeds of greatness stirring inside, but every circumstance says, "There's no way. It's too late." But just as with Moses, God is still going to do what He promised you. It may not have happened yet, but don't worry. It's coming together. God is still on the throne. He sent me to be your burning bush and to let you know that it's not too late. You haven't missed your destiny, and you haven't seen your best days. What God started in your life, He's going to finish. You're about to see a divine coming together. That means it's supernatural. You couldn't make it happen. You didn't have the strength, the talent, or the funds. God set the bush on fire. God healed you. God sent the right people. God brought your dream to pass.

In the Scripture, Jacob thought his son Joseph was dead. Joseph's brothers had brought his bloody robe and told their father that Joseph had been killed by a wild animal. The truth is that they had sold Joseph into slavery. Jacob was so heartbroken, so devastated, that he thought he couldn't go on after losing his favorite son. Year after year went by, and Jacob became an old man. Then suddenly the same brothers who'd sold Joseph brought Jacob the news that he was still alive and in charge of the nation of Egypt. Jacob was overwhelmed. When they took him to see Joseph, he said, "I never thought I would see your face again. But not only did I get to see you, I got to see my grandchildren." When God brings it all together, it's not going to be what you thought. It's going to be bigger, better, and more rewarding than you ever expected. As with Jacob, you're not going to die without seeing your promise fulfilled. Don't stop believing. God is working behind the scenes.

He's already arranged exactly what you need. Now do your part. Get up every day and prophesy life to those dead areas. If you do this, I believe and declare that your dream is coming together, your health is coming together, your relationship is coming together. You're about to hear a noise, a rattling sound. God is going to make happen what you couldn't make happen. As with Ezekiel, you're going to see a great coming together.

> *Get up every day and prophesy life to those dead areas.*

CHAPTER EIGHT

Your Time Is Coming

It's good to have dreams and goals that we're believing for. We should be standing in faith, believing that problems will turn around, but after it's been a long time and we don't see anything improving, it's easy to get discouraged and think it wasn't meant to be. But just because you've given up doesn't mean that God has given up. God doesn't abort dreams. The delays, the detours, and the disappointments don't stop God's plan. What He started in your life, He's going to finish. The Scripture says, "What God has purposed, who can annul it?" It may seem as though what you're believing for could never come to pass, that it's too late, that the odds are against you. God is saying, "Your time is coming." He has not forgotten about you. He has seen the lonely nights. He's seen the unfair situations, the times when you're doing the right thing and not getting the credit, when the illness isn't improving, when your child isn't doing better. Voices whisper, "It will never change." Don't believe the lie. Healing is coming, promotion is coming, and freedom is coming. God has already put it on the schedule. The date has already been ordained.

Psalm 102 says, "There is a set time for favor." You keep honoring God, doing the right thing, and you're going to come into

> *If you could see what God has on your calendar, you wouldn't worry about the client you lost, you wouldn't lose sleep over the family member, you wouldn't be discouraged over the legal situation.*

some of your set times. You will see times when God will show out in your life, times when you will see explosive blessings. You were struggling in your finances, you didn't see how you could get ahead, and suddenly you're promoted, suddenly your business takes off, suddenly you get the position. The medical report says that you'll never get well, but suddenly your health turns around. Suddenly you break the addiction. Suddenly your child gets back on course. What happened? You came into your set time. If you could see what God has on your calendar, you wouldn't worry about the client you lost, you wouldn't lose sleep over the family member, you wouldn't be discouraged over the legal situation.

You may have some obstacles that are not changing even though you're praying and believing. But instead of complaining and living discouraged, all through

> *You didn't miss your chance. You wouldn't be alive if God didn't have something amazing in your future.*

the day you have to say, "Father, thank You that my time is coming. I'm not moved by what I see. I'm moved by what I know. I know that You've already set the time to favor me. You've already set the time to heal me. You've already set the time to turn this around." Get your hopes up. It's not too late. You didn't miss your chance. You wouldn't be alive if God didn't have something amazing in your future.

Anointed Before You're Appointed

David was seventeen years old when the prophet Samuel came to his house to choose one of his father's sons as the next king of Israel. David had seven older brothers. They were bigger, taller, and had more experience. David's father, Jesse, didn't even bother to bring David in from the shepherds' fields. He didn't think that David was king material. "He's too small, too young, and not as talented as his brothers." But Samuel looked over the other brothers and said, "It's none of these. Do you have another son?" Jesse had David come in from the fields. When Samuel saw him, he said, "He's the next king of Israel." People judge by the outside, by your appearance, your nationality, your education, but God looks at the heart. Don't be discouraged if people write you off. Promotion doesn't come from people; it comes from God. He sees that you have a heart after Him. He sees your sincerity, your integrity, your spirit of excellence. What's inside is more powerful than what's on the outside.

> *He sees your sincerity, your integrity, your spirit of excellence. What's inside is more powerful than what's on the outside.*

David was anointed by Samuel to be the next king, but he didn't go to the palace. He went back to the shepherds' fields where he was before and took care of his father's sheep. He was anointed before he was appointed. David knew that big things were in him. He knew that he was going to leave his mark, but month after month he was stuck in the lonely shepherds' fields, doing what seemed like a menial job—feeding sheep, cleaning up their waste, shoveling manure. He could have thought, *God, You said I would be king. You had Samuel anoint me. Why am I still stuck out here?*

I have so much more in me. But David understood this principle that his time was coming. What God promised was already on the schedule. The date had already been set.

Even though David was doing a menial job, he kept doing his best. Nobody was watching him. He didn't have a supervisor. He wasn't clocking in. He could have slacked off and done just enough to get by. But David went the extra mile to watch over the sheep. He fought off wild animals, kept them from harm, made sure they had food and water and were healthy. He had a spirit of excellence. Because he proved to God that he would be faithful taking care of sheep, God trusted him to take care of His people. If you're not faithful in the wilderness, how can God trust you to be faithful in the palace?

As with David, most of the time you will be anointed before you're appointed. You'll have the promise, the dream, the calling, but you won't go straight to the throne. You'll go back to the shepherds' fields. How you respond when you're anointed but not appointed will determine whether you make it to the palace. You have to be your best right where you are. You may have bigger things in you. You know you're going to lead a department at work, or you're going to teach the class, or you're going to run the business. The promise is in your heart. You've been anointed, so to speak, but you're doing something much smaller than what's in you. Will you give it your all even though you're overqualified for that position? Will you serve others even though you have more experience? If you pass the test of being faithful in the small, God will trust you with much.

> *How you respond when you're anointed but not appointed will determine whether you make it to the palace.*

The Blessing Comes Looking for You

Saul was the king of Israel. He struggled with bouts of depression, with tormenting spirits that came against him. His staff told him that when these attacks came, he needed someone to play music and it would help him feel better. Saul agreed and asked them to find someone. They said, "We know a young man named David, the son of Jesse. He's excellent in playing the harp." The Scripture says that Saul sent a message to Jesse saying, "Send me your son David, the shepherd." Here David had been overlooked and felt as though he was forgotten. People discounted him, and his father didn't believe in him, but now the king was asking for him by name. People don't determine your destiny. Someone may have put you at a disadvantage, but keep doing the right thing and your time is coming. Promotion will come calling your name. Opportunity will come looking for you. The right people will come tracking you down. God knows how to vindicate you. He knows how to cause you to stand out.

Imagine Jesse hearing a knock on the door. He answers it, and there stand the king's right-hand men dressed in their military uniforms, some in their armor. Jesse thought, *What in the world are you doing at my house? Am I in trouble? Have I done something wrong?* The main man speaks up and says, "King Saul wants your son David to come and serve him in the palace." Nobody in David's family had paid any attention to him. They didn't give him any credit, but

> In one moment he went from the background to the foreground, from being discounted to being admired.

now the king was calling for him. I'm sure Jesse nearly passed out. Word quickly spread throughout the neighborhood: "The king asked David to come work for him." Now David was the talk of the town. He was suddenly esteemed, honored, looked up to. In one moment he went from the background to the foreground, from being discounted to being admired.

You may have had unfair things happen. Maybe people left you out or tried to discredit you. God saw what happened. He's keeping the records. He hasn't forgotten about you. It may seem as though you're falling behind. You think you can never reach your dreams now, that it's too late. You've been stuck out in the shepherds' fields for too long. No, your time is coming. Keep doing the right thing when the wrong thing is happening. Keep being good to people who are not being good to you. You're going to come into one of these set times when God catapults you ahead. Sometimes God does things gradually, little by little, but there are moments when God will thrust you twenty years ahead. He'll not only make up for lost time, but He'll accelerate things. Overnight, David went from working in the shepherds' fields, the lowest position, to working with the king, the highest position. He didn't have to make it happen, try to manipulate things, or talk people into helping him. The king sent for him.

> *He didn't have to make it happen, try to manipulate things, or talk people into helping him. The king sent for him.*

As with David, you're going to see opportunities that come looking for you that put you years down the road. You're going to think, *How did I get here? I didn't have the qualifications. I wasn't next in line. This should have taken my whole life.* But God is going to suddenly thrust you ahead. Get ready for some set times of acceleration.

Richly Rewarded

The book of Hebrews says, "Don't cast away your confidence, for it will be richly rewarded." It's easy to hear this and think, *Joel, this is never going to happen for me. I've had a lot of bad breaks. I have big obstacles in my path. I'm way behind where I should be.* That kind of thinking is going to limit your life. That's casting away your confidence. God is saying, "Your time is coming. I'm about to do something unusual, something uncommon. I'm going to thrust you ahead. I'm going to free you from the addiction you've struggled with for years. I'm going to vindicate you and pay you back for the wrongs you've suffered. I'm going to take you from insignificant and mediocre to influential and powerful." Now, you have to get in agreement with God. You have to start thanking Him that your time is coming, talking as though it's going to happen, believing that it's on the way. That's what it means to not cast away your confidence.

When you do this, God promises that you will be richly rewarded. Look at how good God is. To just be rewarded would be fine, but God will exceed your expectations. He'll make things happen that you didn't see coming. Now don't get talked out of your dreams. You may feel like David did, that you're stuck out in the shepherds' fields and nobody pays attention to your gifts. You're in prime position to be catapulted to a new level. People may not pay attention, but God sees you. He's the one who matters. He controls the universe. He has already sched-

> *To just be rewarded would be fine, but God will exceed your expectations.*

uled your set times of favor, set times of healing, set times of acceleration. There are moments in your future that are going to cause you to stand out, moments that will catapult you to a new level, moments when favor will come looking for you.

There's a young man who attends Lakewood. He had a dream to become a physician and graduated from college with honors. He applied to forty medical schools, but only three schools contacted him back. He interviewed with them, but he was turned down. He was so disappointed. This was what he'd always wanted to do. He had put all of his time, energy, and focus into getting into medical school, but now that door had closed. He didn't understand it. He had worked so hard. But instead of being sour, he kept believing that his time was coming. He knew that God didn't bring him this far to leave him. When things happen that aren't fair, when you don't understand, you have to trust that God is still in control and that He knows what's best for you. His ways are not our ways. He doesn't always take us down the path that we thought. There will be times when doors close that don't make sense, when people who should be for us are not around, and when we're doing the right thing but the wrong thing keeps happening. None of that is a surprise to God. He's already lined up the breaks you need—the open doors, the right people, the healing, the baby. It's already on your schedule.

> *He doesn't always take us down the path that we thought.*

This young man attended a seminar for students who wanted to get into medical school. One option they mentioned was working for the armed services. When he heard that, something ignited inside. He knew that's what he wanted to do. He met a gentleman there who took an interest in him and went out of his way to put in a good word for him. This time the young man received news that he was accepted with a full scholarship for the armed forces medical school. He would not only have no cost for his medical education, but he would be paid a substantial salary while he attended school. What happened? He came into one of his set times. If God had not closed the other doors, if a school would have accepted him earlier, he would never have seen this opportunity that was more than he could imagine. He never dreamed he would be paid the whole time and come out of medical school with no debt.

If you won't cast away your confidence, God will richly reward you. You may have gone through some disappointments, things didn't turn out the way you hoped, but you don't know what God is up to. The reason He closed the other doors is because He has something better. Don't be discouraged by what didn't work out. Stay in faith. Your time is coming. The right opportunity is on the way. It's going to be better than you thought. If someone walked out of your life, it may have been unfair and painful, but it didn't stop your destiny. They left only to make room for someone better. God has beauty for those ashes. You haven't seen your best days. Keep moving forward when you don't understand. Keep being your best when it's not fair.

> *The reason He closed the other doors is because He has something better.*

Suddenly

This is what Joseph did in the Scripture. Year after year, how could he have a good attitude after being betrayed by his brothers, sold into slavery, and put into prison for something that he didn't do? Deep down he knew his time was coming. He knew that what God spoke to him as a teenager, the dream that was put in his heart, would come to pass. He didn't know how, when, or where. All he knew was that God is faithful and that the set time was already on the calendar. He didn't cast away his confidence even though he had a lot of bad breaks and plenty of opportunities to give up. But when you understand that God is ordering your steps, that nothing can happen to you without His permission, you won't fall apart when an illness hits. You won't live bitter when someone does you wrong. You won't give up on your dream when life throws you a curve. You know it's all a part of God's plan. That setback is only setting you up to go further. God had the solution before you had the problem. He's already set the time to turn it around, set the time to open the right door, set the time to bring you out promoted, vindicated, healthy and whole.

> *He's already set the time to turn it around, set the time to open the right door, set the time to bring you out promoted, vindicated, healthy and whole.*

One day, Pharaoh, the ruler of Egypt, did not understand the meaning of a dream that he had. The Scripture says, "Pharaoh sent for Joseph. He was hastily brought from the dungeon into Pharaoh's presence." Just as King Saul had said, "Send me the shepherd named David to the palace," Pharaoh said, "Send me the prisoner who interprets dreams, send me the slave named Joseph." Both times the promotion came looking for them. You don't have to look for the blessing; the blessing is going to come looking for you. Joseph was brought to the palace hastily. He wasn't expecting it. It had been an ordinary day in the prison, nothing special, and suddenly he was in the palace. He didn't see it coming. There wasn't any sign of it. He woke up a slave in prison, and he went to bed that night the prime minister. God has some of these "suddenlies" in

> *God has some of these "suddenlies" in your future.*

your future. You don't see anything improving, everything looks the same, but you come into a set time. It's going to happen hastily, in a hurry, and quickly things turn around, quickly the door opens, quickly your health improves.

It may be difficult now, but at any moment you could get a call as Joseph did. "Send me Julie, send me William, send me Maria." That's how you stay in faith. You have to keep this hope in your heart, knowing that God has already lined up these set times for you. If you only look at your situation in the natural, you'll get discouraged, because God puts dreams in our hearts that we can't accomplish on our own. We don't have the resources, the connections, or the experience. He does this so we have to depend on Him. We face challenges that we can't overcome by ourselves. It might be a sickness, an addiction, or people who are more powerful. It looks as though we're stuck, but deep down you have to know that the forces for you are greater than the forces against you. You may feel outnumbered and at a disadvantage. The sickness seems bigger, the addiction stronger. Keep reminding yourself that your time is coming. One touch of God's favor, one set time, and things will suddenly change. Nothing can stand against our God. No sickness is too great, no addiction too strong, and no enemy too powerful.

> *If you only look at your situation in the natural, you'll get discouraged, because God puts dreams in our hearts that we can't accomplish on our own.*

Light Comes Bursting In

I talked with a young man who had been diagnosed with terminal brain cancer. The doctors gave him only eighteen months to live. He heard me tell how my mother quoted healing Scriptures when she was sick with cancer and how she had defied the odds. Instead of accepting the diagnosis and thinking his life was over, he started quoting these Scriptures and thanking God that He was restoring health to him. The psalmist says, "When darkness overtakes the righteous, light will come bursting in." When you're in a tough time, when the odds are against you, it seems as though there's no way out. It's easy to live worried and fall apart, but you have to remind yourself that God has already set the time for light to come bursting in. He's already set the time for healing, set the time for breakthroughs.

Bursting means it's going to happen suddenly. You didn't see it coming. You can't explain it. It's out of the ordinary. When I spoke with this man who had cancer, he said that he had just come to the end of the eighteen months. That's how much time he was given to live. When he went back to the hospital for a checkup, the doctors said, "We can't explain this, we don't know how it happened, but we can't find any cancer in your brain. You are perfectly well." When you come into your set time, God will make things happen that you couldn't make happen. He can do what medicine cannot do. He's not limited by what limits us. We're natural; He's supernatural.

> *When you come into your set time, God will make things happen that you couldn't make happen.*

You may be in a time of darkness. Instead of complaining

about the darkness, being depressed by the darkness, try a different approach and say, "Father, thank You that Your light is about to come bursting in. Thank You that my set time for favor, set time for healing, set time for deliverance is on the way." Don't cast away your confidence. God is bigger than what you're facing. You may not see how it can work out. Logically, there's no way. The good news is that you don't have to figure it out. All you have to do is believe. When you believe, all things are possible. Do as this man did and go through the day saying, "Father, I don't see a way, but I know You have a way. It doesn't look possible to me, but I know You can do the impossible." You'll see these times when God will show out in your life. It may not have happened yet, but I believe you are closer than you think. You are close to your breakthrough. You are close to seeing things turn around. You are close to your child getting back on course. You wouldn't be reading this if you weren't about to see one of your set times.

Believe the Promise

In 1 Samuel 1, there was a young wife named Hannah who was barren, unable to have children. Hannah kept praying and believing, but the Scripture says, "The Lord had shut her womb." To make matters worse, her husband was also married to another woman named Peninnah, who had baby after baby. This other wife would make fun of Hannah, trying to make her feel as though she was inferior, that something was wrong with her. Hannah would end up feeling hurt and in tears. It didn't seem fair. The good news is that the same God who shuts wombs can open wombs. Just as God shuts doors, He can open doors. Year after year went by with no sign of a baby, and Hannah was very discouraged. She went to the temple, fell on her knees and began to weep, asking God to give her a child. The high priest Eli saw how distraught she was and asked what was wrong. She explained that she couldn't have children and she was asking God to open her womb. Eli said, "Cheer up. The God of Israel has granted your request. You're going to have a baby." He was saying, "You're about to come into one of your set times. You're about to see God do something that you've never seen." Here's the key: Hannah believed what he said. She went back home a different person. She had a smile on her face and a spring in her step even though she didn't have her baby yet. All she had was the promise that her time was coming. A year later, she was holding her baby boy named Samuel in her arms.

Sometimes, as with Hannah and the other wife, it seems as though everybody is being blessed except you. Everybody is getting married except you. Everybody is seeing promotion except you. It's as though the favor has been shut off. But don't be discouraged by what hasn't happened yet. Your time is coming. Your baby is coming, your healing is coming, your joy is coming. God is about to open your womb, so to speak. You're about to see things for which you've been believing for a long time. You're going to see the fulfillment of promises that you thought would never happen, of dreams that you've let go of. You are close to your set time of favor.

> *Don't be discouraged by what hasn't happened yet. Your time is coming.*

Now, I've done what Eli did. I've announced what God said. You have to do as Hannah did and say, "Yes, God. This is for me." Let this seed take root in your spirit. Don't let it just be another encouraging message. Let it ignite your faith. Let it come alive inside. You are on the verge of seeing God do something amazing. It's not far off in the distance. You are close to your breakthrough. You are in the final stretch. Now don't cast away your confidence. This is not the time to get discouraged or to talk defeat. This is the time to stir up your faith, to turn up your praise, to talk like it's en route. All through the day you have to say, "Father, thank You that my time is coming. Thank You that You're the way maker, the promise keeper, the miracle worker." If you do this, God says that you will be richly rewarded. I believe and declare that light is about to come bursting in. God is about to surprise you. He's going to do something that you've never seen, something that will thrust you to a new level. Negative situations are about to suddenly turn around. Get ready. The right people, healing, breakthroughs, and vindication are coming. As with Joseph and David and Hannah, blessing is going to come looking for you.

CHAPTER NINE

Yes Is Coming

Sometimes we've gone through so many noes that we get discouraged and give up on our dreams. Maybe the loan didn't go through, you didn't get the promotion, or you tried to break the addiction but you couldn't do it. A young couple told me how they've had four miscarriages and haven't been able to have a baby. You may have had a lot of noes in the past, your dreams haven't come true yet, but I believe God is saying, "This is going to be a season of yes—yes to the healing, yes to the promotion, yes to the breakthrough, yes to having that baby." What hasn't worked out in the past is suddenly going to fall into place. Doors you thought were closed are suddenly going to open. Dreams you've given up on, promises you've let go of and thought, *There's no way,* God is about to make a way. In this season of yes, God is going to reverse the noes. The times when you've been denied, turned down, and told, "No, thanks," were not the end; they just weren't the right time. Yes is coming. Yes to the dream you quit pursuing, yes to the child getting back on the right course, yes to the business you've been wanting to start.

Now, people may tell you, "No, you can't get well. Look at the medical report. No, sorry, you don't have the experience we need.

> *The times when you've been denied, turned down, and told, "No, thanks," were not the end; they just weren't the right time.*

No, you're not talented enough. No, that idea's not going to work for us." Their no doesn't cancel out God's yes. Don't let them talk you out of your dreams. God has the final say. He's saying, "Get ready for yes. Yes to increase. Yes to freedom from the addiction. Yes to seeing your family restored. Yes to new opportunities."

God is going to put you in the right place at the right time. He's going to send divine connections, people who will go out of their way to be good to you. You couldn't make it happen. It is the favor of God bringing you into your yes.

The Season of Yes

I talked to a lady who had been out of work for over a year. She worked as a sales executive and had been very successful. After many years, unexpectedly her contract was not renewed. She had an impressive résumé and applied to a couple of dozen companies, but no one was interested. She was turned down again and again. Several months later, a company called and asked her to come in for an interview. She was excited. It looked as though something had finally opened up, and the interview went well. She thought she had it, but they called back and said she just wasn't the right fit. That was followed by four more interviews, where she went in and it went well, it looked as though she was the frontrunner, then she was told no—it was one no after another. A few months later, a company in another state called. They were very interested and said the final decision was between her and one man. She flew to that city for an interview. On the way to the office, the friendly taxicab driver struck up a conversation with her. She told him that she was on her way to a job interview and how she'd been praying and believing that something would open up. She said that out of all the offers she'd had, this was the one she wanted the most. The driver dropped her off and told her that he was pulling for her and that he believed she was going to get it.

Later that day, the woman who did the job interview with this lady had to catch a plane. It just so happened that the same taxicab driver was sent to the office and picked her up. Being the friendly driver that he was, he asked her how her day was going. She explained how she had interviewed two people, a man and a woman, for a sales position and couldn't decide between the two. He said, "Let me tell you who you should pick." She asked, "What do you mean?" He replied, "I picked up the lady you interviewed and brought her to your office this morning. You won't find a better person. She's smart, she's talented, she's articulate, plus she really wants to work for you." He went on and on, singing her praises. The woman said, "You know what? I just made my decision." When she called the lady in the other state and told her that she had gotten the position, she said, "If you ever see that taxicab driver again, you need to thank him because he's the reason I chose you."

What are the chances in a large city that the same taxicab driver would pick up both women? That wasn't a coincidence; that was the hand of God. In this season of yes, God is going to have the right people put in a good word for you. You may not think you have the connections. Don't worry. You have friends in high places. God is not only guiding and directing your

> *What are the chances in a large city that the same taxicab driver would pick up both women?*

steps, He's lining up the people you need. He's arranging things in your favor.

Your Yes with God's Yes

The apostle Paul says in 2 Corinthians 1, "Whatever God has promised gets stamped with yes." That means the dreams God's placed in your heart, the promises He's spoken over you, have already been stamped with yes. God has already set the date to bring it to pass. It's already on the schedule. But there's one more thing God needs. Paul goes on to say, "God's yes with our yes together make it a sure thing." God is saying yes. Now He needs your yes to make it happen. God's yes by itself is not enough. God works where there's faith. If this lady would have gone around thinking, *Oh, I'll never get the position. Nothing good ever happens to me*, that would have kept it from happening.

> *The dreams God's placed in your heart, the promises He's spoken over you, have already been stamped with yes.*

When it comes to God, be a yes man, be a yes woman. God says He's restoring health to you. You can think of all the reasons why you're not going to get well, or you can be a yes man. "Yes, God. I agree. Thank You that I'm getting healthier. Thank You that I'm getting stronger." God says in Psalm 65 that He's going to crown your year with a bountiful harvest. You can go around not expecting good breaks, not expecting to get ahead, or you can be a yes woman. "Yes, God. I agree. Thank You that it's going to be a blessed, prosperous, abundant, bountiful year." That's not just being positive, that's putting your yes with God's yes. God says what was meant for your harm He's going to turn and use to your advantage. You can dwell on all your hurts, what didn't work out, and the people who did you wrong, or you can be a yes man. "Yes, God. I agree. Thank You for beauty for these ashes. Thank You that You're my vindicator. Thank You that You're fighting my battles."

Is God waiting for your yes? Are you letting the noes, the disappointments, and the delays convince you that it's not going to happen? You may not have seen it yet, but this is a new day. You are coming into a season of yes. I'm asking you to put your yes with God's yes and watch what happens.

> *Is God waiting for your yes?*

A No Turned into a Yes

In the previous chapter, I described the story of how after Hannah had been barren for several years, she went to the temple, started weeping in anguish and asking God to give her a baby. When the high priest Eli announced to her that the God of Israel had granted her request for a baby, she went back home feeling like a different person. Even though on the outside, nothing had changed, she had put her yes with God's yes. There was no baby, no sign of a child, but at that point, she believed she was going to have a baby. When the other wife made fun of her—"Too bad, Hannah. You'll never have a child"—instead of getting upset, instead of crying, her new attitude was: *I may have had some noes, but I have some inside information. I know my yes is coming. The God of Israel has spoken it over me. I may not see it yet, but I walk by faith and not by sight. I know my baby is coming.*

A year later, Hannah was holding her baby boy, Samuel, in her arms. She came into her yes. As with Hannah, you may have had a lot of noes. People have tried to discourage you, make you think it's never going to happen. You need to get ready. Your yes is coming. The same God who shut Hannah's womb opened Hannah's womb. God may have said no in the past, but that doesn't mean it's going to be no in the future. Just as God turned Hannah's no into a yes, God is going to turn around some noes for you. Will you do as Hannah did and start acting as though what God told you is going to happen? All Hannah had was a word from the high priest that she was going to have a baby. She didn't have an ultrasound. She didn't have a pregnancy test. She just had what Eli said to her. He could have been wrong.

> *God may have said no in the past, but that doesn't mean it's going to be no in the future.*

You have something so much more powerful. You have the promise from the God who spoke worlds into existence. He's saying, "If you put your yes with My yes, I'll turn the noes around." You have situations that seem permanent. Maybe it's an addiction you've dealt with for years, or a health issue that won't go away, or a struggle in your finances. It seems as though you're stuck. Thoughts tell you, *Just accept the noes. Just get used to it.* Don't believe those lies. God is about to open up your womb, so to speak. You need to get ready. What you've been dreaming about—the child to get back on course, the business to take off, the person to spend your life with—is coming. Your yes is headed your way.

The Dream Is Stamped with Yes

I know a lady who was in her early twenties working as a news reporter. She had a really bad case of rosacea, a skin condition that causes blushing and flushing and visible blood vessels in your face. When she was out filming a report, if she sweated or accidentally touched her face or rubbed her makeup off, that red would shine through so brightly and looked bad. She couldn't find any makeup that would cover it up and last. It was such a problem that she ended up quitting her job as a news reporter. She determined she would create a new makeup line that would fix her problem, and she developed a product that she really liked. She believed it would be a commercial success. She and her husband went to bank after bank, trying to get funding, but they were turned down again and again. Her husband created a website so people could order the product, but after it was up for weeks and weeks, there was no activity, no orders. Finally, an order came through. She went running to her husband and exclaimed, "Look, we got our first order!" He replied, "No, that was me. I was just testing the website."

This lady knew that God had put this dream in her heart, but all she kept getting were noes. Her goal was to somehow get on a home shopping channel such as QVC. For years she sent her product to the different channels. She met with a sales representative to try to make it happen, but it didn't work out. Finally, this couple was down to their last one thousand dollars and didn't know what they were going to do. She decided to go to a large cosmetic convention. All the major companies were there, and she rented a tiny three-foot booth where she was displaying her product. Across the way, QVC had a huge booth. During the convention, an older lady approached her and said, "Honey, I love your product. I'm going to tell my buyers at QVC that we need to have you on our channel."

That lady was an on-air personality who had been there for over seventeen years. She used her influence to open the door. When this young lady went on QVC, her product was a huge hit. Our friend, Jamie Kern Lima, the cofounder of IT Cosmetics, sold her products on more than 1,000 live shows on QVC and built the largest beauty brand in their history. She eventually sold IT Cosmetics to L'Oréal and became the first female CEO in L'Oréal's one hundred year history.

But as with Hannah, for years it was as if the womb was shut up for Jamie. There were no good breaks, no favor, very little progress. Then one day she came into her yes. That one good break thrust her further than she ever imagined. Years later, she was talking to the lady who put in a good word for her that day and she asked her why she did it. The lady answered, "Well, I liked your product, but it wasn't about the cosmetics. When I saw you that day, I felt as though God said to me, 'Go and help that young lady.'"

That one good break thrust her further than she ever imagined.

God has the right people lined up for you. In this season of yes, you're going to see doors open that you haven't been able to open for years. The dream that God has placed in your heart has already been stamped with yes. Are you adding your yes to God's yes? Are you doing as Hannah did and thanking God, even though you don't see anything happening? Will you be bold enough to believe that you're still going to give birth, even though it feels as though your womb has been shut? Heaven is saying yes—yes to your dream, yes to your healing, yes to the freedom, yes to the breakthrough.

"Well, Joel, this sounds good. It's encouraging, but I don't think I'm going to have a season of yes. I've had so many noes." You're right where Hannah was. The problem is that if you keep adding your no to God's yes, you can cancel out what God has in store. Other people's no cannot stop you. What they say and what they do has no control over your destiny. The enemy's no cannot stop you. What you believe is what matters. God needs your yes. He has amazing things in your future. He's going to give you more influence and favor than you've ever imagined. Now keep adding the yes. Thoughts may tell you *no*. Circumstances may tell you it's never going to happen, but your yes and God's yes make it a sure thing. Why? Because God controls the universe. One touch of His favor can turn a no into a yes. You'll go from "No, we don't need you" to "Yes, you have the position." You'll go from "No, you'll never get well"

> *What you believe is what matters. God needs your yes.*

to "Good news. You're cancer-free." You'll go from interview to interview with no success to having a taxicab driver put in a good word for you. You need to get ready. Your yes is on the way. As it was with Hannah, God is about to open up your womb.

When God Says No

In the book of 2 Kings, there was a king named Hezekiah who was told no. But his no didn't come from people, it came from God. He was very sick, close to death. His mentor, the prophet Isaiah, came to the palace to see him. Isaiah is known as the eagle-eyed prophet because he could see and hear what God had for His people in the future. He was the one who spoke for God, and he didn't make mistakes. I can imagine when King Hezekiah heard the news that Isaiah had come into the palace, he brightened up, thinking, *Maybe there's hope. Maybe he's going to pray for me, and I'm going to get well. Or maybe he'll give me an encouraging word that I can stand on.* Isaiah came in and said, "King Hezekiah, I have a word from the Lord for you." Hezekiah leaned in closer. Isaiah continued, "The Lord says, 'Set your house in order, for you will surely die.'" He didn't say, "You might die. Hezekiah, it doesn't look too good, but maybe you'll pull through." Isaiah said, "You will surely die," and he walked out.

What do you do when God says no? Hezekiah could have thought, *Well, too bad for me. I'm done. There's no use even trying.* But the Scripture says Hezekiah turned his face to the wall and started praying. He reminded God how he had served Him, how he'd torn down the pagan altars, and how he'd set a new standard for his family. He asked God in His mercy to give him more years.

> *If you dare do as Hezekiah did and ask God for the yes, your faith can cause God to change His mind.*

His attitude was: *If I die, I'm going to die asking for the yes.* Before Isaiah could leave the palace grounds, God said to him, "Isaiah, go back to Hezekiah and tell him I've heard his prayers and I've changed my mind. I'm going to add fifteen years to his life." Even when you feel as though God has said no, if you dare do as Hezekiah did and ask God for the yes, your faith can cause God to change His mind.

In this season of yes, God is going to reverse some noes. God is going to correct some of the mistakes that you've made and give you another chance. He's going to bring opportunities that you've missed back across your path. Things that have been a struggle, with constant pressure, are going to suddenly turn around. Both Hezekiah and Hannah faced situations where God said no. God shut Hannah's womb, and He told Hezekiah that he was done.

> *The common denominator was they both asked for yes in the face of no.*

Hannah went to the temple and asked for a baby. Hezekiah asked for more years. The common denominator was they both asked for yes in the face of no. Every circumstance said, "Forget it. God said no. Just live with it." Their attitude was: *God, we know You control the universe. Even though this seems like a no to us, we're asking for Your great mercy to change Your mind and give us a yes.* Are you bold enough to ask for a yes, even though all you keep getting are noes?

How Badly Do You Want It?

Jesus told a parable in Luke 18 about a widow who went to see a judge to try to get relief from someone who had done her harm. He was an unjust judge. He wasn't fair with her, didn't listen to her, and wouldn't give her the time of day. He just dismissed her and sent her away. The next day, the widow was right back in his courtroom, asking for justice. The judge said, "Lady, didn't I tell you no yesterday?" She answered, "Yes, you did. But I'm not going to leave you alone until you give me a yes." He had her put out again, but she came back the next day and the next and the next, asking for justice, pleading her case. Finally, the judge got so frustrated that he said, "This woman is driving me crazy. I'm going to see that she gets justice, because she is wearing me down with her constant requests!" She kept asking for yes in the face of no.

If you're going to see your yes, you have to be determined. If you accept the first no, you weren't serious about it. The noes are a test. God wants to see how badly you want it. If you get discouraged and give up, you didn't want it badly enough. You have to do as this woman did and keep

Keep asking, keep praying, keep believing, keep dreaming, keep hoping.

asking, keep praying, keep believing, keep dreaming, keep hoping. If one door closes, try another door. If one company says no, try another company. If one bank turns you down, try another bank.

A friend of mine was trying to get the financing to start his business. He was turned down by thirty-one banks in a row. Thirty-one times he was told, "No, sorry. We can't help you. It doesn't seem like a good idea to us." He knew that dream had already been stamped with God's yes. He just kept adding his yes, going from closed door to closed door, not getting discouraged. Bank number thirty-two said, "We think it's a great idea." He started his business, which has taken off and expanded all around the world. He told me how some of those same banks now are trying to get his account. You know what he tells them? No.

What am I saying? Don't get discouraged by the noes. The noes are a part of your destiny. They're leading you to the yes. You have to come to your closed doors before you get to your open doors. You may have had a lot of noes in the past; things haven't worked out. You need to get ready. Your yes is coming. God is going to open doors that you could not open. He's going to cause people to change their mind and go out of their way to be good to you. It's going to be unprecedented favor. You will know it is the hand of God.

> *The noes are a part of your destiny. They're leading you to the yes.*

You Are the History Maker

In Chapter Six, I introduced the story of a single mom named Sherree who raised her son, EJayy, in Compton, California, which is known for being a rough environment, with drugs and gun violence. Despite her husband being in the federal penitentiary, and despite being surrounded by countless negative influences, Sherree was believing and praying for EJayy to be able to go to college. Even though the odds were against him, they believed that God would open the right doors. They'd had a lot of noes in the past, but they knew their yes was coming. They knew that God was going to do something unusual, something out of the ordinary. When EJayy received the good news that he had been accepted into Harvard University, he made history in Compton. You may have heard the phrase "Straight out of Compton," which speaks of the negative, the gangs, the violence. How about a new phrase: "Straight out of Compton, and straight to Harvard"?

Jesus came from the city of Nazareth, which was a poor, run-down city in those days. It was a somewhat secluded, isolated city that had a bad reputation for its morality. His critics said, "Can any good thing come out of Nazareth?" It was not an important, influential place, yet the Son of God came out of Nazareth. Can any good thing come out of Compton? Yes, EJayy. Yes, Sherree. Yes, a whole lot of others. Can any good thing come out of your neighborhood? Yes, you can. You're the history maker. You're the exception. You have seeds of greatness. As with EJayy and Sherree, there are yesses in your future that are going to thrust you to the next level. God is going to open doors that no man can shut. He's going to bring divine connections, people

> *Can any good thing come out of your neighborhood? Yes, you can.*

who will use their influence to push you into your purpose. You may have had a lot of noes in the past, but you need to get ready. I believe and declare you are coming into your season of yes. God is saying yes to the scholarship, yes to the right person, yes to the healing, yes to the breakthrough. Your yes is on the way.

CHAPTER TEN

Ease Is Coming

We all go through seasons of struggle when we're doing the right thing but it feels like it's uphill. There's pressure raising the children. We're believing for our health to improve, but it's not getting better. We're working hard, but it seems as though we're taking one step forward and two steps back. Too often we lose our enthusiasm and think this is just the way life is. In Matthew 11, Jesus talks about how the kingdom of Heaven suffers violence and you have to take it by force. He was telling us that there will be seasons where you have to stand strong and fight the good fight of faith. But a few verses later in that same chapter, He says, "My yoke is easy and My burden is light." He was saying, "You're going to go through times of struggle, strain, and difficulty, but don't get discouraged. That's not permanent. My yoke, what I'm going to put on you, is easy, and My burden is light."

You may be struggling now, and you feel pressured. Maybe you think that's the way it's always going to be. You're thinking you'll always struggle in your health, your finances, or your relationships. No, get ready. You're about to come into an anointing of ease. When you come into this ease, what used to be a struggle will not be a struggle anymore. There's going to be a supernatural

> *There's going to be a supernatural grace, a favor that lightens the load and takes the pressure off.*

grace, a favor that lightens the load and takes the pressure off. God says that He will go before you and make your crooked places straight. That means He's going to smooth things out. He's going to make your life easier. You're coming into a season where things are going to fall into place. You're going to get breaks that you didn't see coming. Problems that you thought were permanent are about to turn around. You're not going to go through life struggling, pressured, weighed down by challenges. This is a new day. Ease is coming.

David says, "God anoints my head with oil." Oil makes things flow. Where there's friction, things that are stuck, oil is used to lubricate and make them more fluid. God is going to oil your life. The anointing is going to cause things to be easier. You're going to accomplish more with less work. What has stopped you in the past, caused you friction, is not going to stop you anymore. You're going to flow right past it. You're going to accomplish goals and think, *That was easier than I thought. I never dreamed it would happen that fast.* That's the anointing of ease.

That Was Easy

There's a large company that for many years had as its slogan, "That Was Easy." A few years ago somebody sent me their red button that says "that was easy" when you push it. I keep this button on my bathroom counter next to the sink. Every so often I reach over and hit that button. I like getting that phrase down in my spirit. It's easy to go through life looking at our obstacles, focused on our challenges, and thinking, *This is going to be hard. I dread doing this. I don't think it's ever going to change.* That mind-set not only steals our passion, but it keeps us from seeing God's favor.

When my father died and I first started ministering, it took everything I had to write a message for the next Sunday—all my strength, my creativity, my focus. I was pressured, stressed, and it went down to the wire. When I was done, I felt as though that was the last message I could ever write. If I wasn't careful, I would dread it and think, *I can't do this again. What am I going to say? This is too hard.* I had to turn it around and say, "Father, thank You that Your yoke is easy. Thank You that I am well able. Thank You that You've equipped me and empowered me." I got my mind going in the right direction. I went through seasons of testing and proving, but I didn't let that become permanent in my thinking. One day I came into this anointing of ease. What once was a struggle is not a struggle anymore. Every time I finish a message I hit that button. "That was easy."

> *What once was a struggle is not a struggle anymore.*

Quit telling yourself, "This is too hard. It's never going to work out. I'll never get out of debt. I'll never accomplish my dream." This is a new day. You're going to have a strength you didn't have. You're going to have wisdom, creativity, and favor. God didn't create you to struggle your whole life. His yoke is easy. You may have had that addiction for a long time. It's going to be easier to break than you think. God is giving you a supernatural grace. You're going to look back and say, "That was easy." You've been struggling in your finances, pressured to pay the bills, pressured to get ahead. I declare that pressure is coming to an end. God is going to cause good breaks to find you, new doors are going to open, and your gifts and talents are going to come out in a new way. You're going to say, "That was easy."

The Right People, the Right Breaks, the Right Opportunities

Two years after I wrote my first book, *Your Best Life Now*, a man was walking by Madison Square Garden in New York City. He was an executive at one of the largest publishing companies in the world. He saw my name up on the marquee and people lined up to get in. He'd never heard of me, but he went home and did some research. He called my literary agent and said that he wanted to publish my next book. She said, "We already have a publisher, and we're happy." He asked her if he could make an offer. She said, "Sure." He offered an amount more than I ever dreamed. When she called me and told me, I nearly passed out. I said, "You do great work!" She said, "Actually, I didn't go to him. He came to me." I thought to myself, *That was easy.*

That was God lining up the right people, having that man at the right place at the right time. If he had not left work late that night, he wouldn't have seen those people. If he had not taken the train home, he wouldn't have been in that area. If he had been preoccupied, thinking about something else, he could have passed by the arena thinking the line was for a ballgame or a concert. All these things had to fall perfectly into place. That was the hand of God making my life easier. God has the right people lined up for you.

> *All these things had to fall perfectly into place.*

He has the right breaks and the right opportunities. You may not have seen it yet, but if you keep honoring God and being your best, He's going to take you into overflow. You're not going to live pressured by bills, pressured to make ends meet, pressured to send your children to college. God is going to do something unusual, unexpected, something you couldn't make happen.

I know a single mom who was working hard, raising her children, trying to make ends meet, but every month she was barely able to pay her bills. She told how she wanted to take a vacation, but every time she had saved extra money, something would break that had to be fixed. She was being her best, but she couldn't get ahead. It looked as though she would struggle her whole life. But when you keep doing the right thing, when you keep passing those tests, you're going to come into this anointing of ease. God is going to make things happen that will take the pressure off. He's going to lighten the load. One day her supervisor unexpectedly took early retirement, and she was given her position. That came with a significant increase in salary. She was very grateful. Several years later, one of the vice presidents of this large company, who was her manager, suddenly resigned, and she was offered that position. Today, this single mom makes more than ten times what she made when she started. She doesn't live under that constant pressure. She can take vacations whenever she wants. She supports other single-parent families. She said, "Joel, I don't even know how it happened. Things just fell into place, and here I am." What she was really saying was, "That was easy." That's what God is going to do for you. He's going to put you at the right place at the right time. He's going to open doors that no man can shut. He's going to cause people to want to be good to you. You may be struggling in some areas now, but don't get discouraged. That's not permanent. Ease is on the way.

> *He's going to cause people to want to be good to you.*

I talked with a young man who was finishing up his masters and had one final exam. It was the hardest class on his schedule. He was very stressed out over it, concerned that he wasn't going to pass. We prayed that God would give him wisdom and help him to excel. He came back the next week so excited that he had passed the test. I said, "How was it?" He said, "It's funny. My classmates thought it was so difficult, but to me it was much easier than I expected. I knew the material. There weren't any surprises. The answers just came to mind." He did his part. He prepared, he studied, then God stepped in and made it easier than expected. Quit thinking, *I'll never pass. I'll never get ahead. This is going to be so hard.* Sometimes we expect to struggle. We expect it to be difficult. Turn it around and say, "Father, thank You for Your anointing of ease. Thank You that You're causing me to succeed. Thank You that blessings are chasing me down." Some of the things that you're dreading, the things that you don't see how they're going to work out, are not going to be what you think. God is going before you and making your crooked places straight. You're going to say as this man did, "It was easier than I thought."

> *Some of the things that you're dreading, the things that you don't see how they're going to work out, are not going to be what you think.*

Your Cows Are Coming

In the book of 1 Samuel, the Philistines had defeated the Israelites in a battle. They also captured the ark of the covenant, which was the place of the presence of God in the midst of His people. The Israelites were distraught. When the elderly high priest Eli heard the news, he fell backward, broke his neck, and died. Eli's two sons were killed in that battle. One of his son's wives was pregnant, and when she found out about his death, she went into labor and gave birth to the baby. She named her son Ichabod, saying, "The Glory has departed from Israel." That was the last thing she said before she passed away. All of Israel was in mourning. They had not only lost the ark of the covenant, but thirty thousand men had been killed in the battle. They didn't have a chance against the Philistines. It looked as though the ark was gone forever.

The Philistines took the ark to their temple and placed it next to their god Dagon, a stone statue that they worshipped. In the middle of the night, Dagon fell over before the ark. They thought it was a coincidence and put Dagon back in his place. The next night he fell over again, but this time his head and hands were broken off. They realized their god couldn't stand in the presence of Israel's God. Then plagues began to break out among the Philistines, with people getting tumors and boils. The Philistines finally realized it was because of the ark of the covenant. They decided to move it to a different city, but the same boils and tumors started afflicting those people. They panicked and said, "We have to get rid of the ark. We can't mess with the God of Israel."

Seven months after the Philistines captured the ark of the covenant, they built a cart, put the ark on it, and hooked it up to two young cows. They loaded the cart up with gifts of gold statues, turned it loose, and let the cows go wherever they wanted. The cows started heading straight toward the Israelite border. In a few days, the Israelites saw the ark coming and couldn't believe their eyes. They

> *They not only got the ark back, but they didn't even have to fight for it.*

never dreamed they would see it again, and they started celebrating. They not only got the ark back, but they didn't even have to fight for it. It came looking for them. If they'd had one of those red buttons, they would have hit it and heard, "That was easy."

During those seven months, I'm sure the Israelites were making plans to attack, coming up with strategies to get the ark back.

They had lost thousands of men, and they knew they would lose many more. They were worried and afraid, but then they saw the cows coming. All of a sudden their lives got much easier. They were so relieved. It's like some of the things you're worried about, trying to figure out how you're going to accomplish your dream, how you're going to get healthy again, how you're going to afford to send your children to college. You're trying to come up with plans and strategies, and that's good. We should do our part, but God is going to do for you what He did for them. He's going to have those things find you. You're not going to have to fight that battle. You're not going to have to go after them. Good breaks are going to come to you. The right people are going to search you out. What you're believing for is going to track you down. God is saying, "Get ready. The cows are coming." What belongs to you is headed your way—the contracts, the promotion, the healing, the spouse, the favor. God is going to make things happen that you could never make happen.

> *What you're believing for is going to track you down.*

Those cows could have stayed where they were grazing, or they could have gone in the opposite direction. But God controls the universe. God controls the cows. He knows how to get what's yours into your hands. People can't stop Him, bad breaks can't stop Him, cows can't stop Him, and enemies can't stop Him. The Philistines took the ark, but they couldn't keep it. When they tried, it made them miserable. In the same way, nobody can keep what belongs to you. The enemy may take your health for a little while, but he can't keep it. It doesn't belong to him. You are God's property. God will make sure your health comes back. The enemy may distract your child and get him off course for a season, but he can't keep him there. Quit worrying. Quit losing sleep. He's coming back. The enemy may have taken your dream temporarily, and you've had some bad breaks and disappointments. Stay encouraged. What has your name on it is going to come looking for you. You might see some cows show up this week. God is going to surprise you. What you thought would never work out and was over and done,

> *You might see some cows show up this week.*

suddenly things are going to fall into place. You don't have to fight. You don't have to struggle. Just get up every morning and say, "Father, thank You that my cows are coming."

A Season of Ease

The prophet Isaiah told the Israelites that "their swords will be turned to plowshares, their spears to pruning hooks." God was saying, "You're coming into a season when you're not going to need your swords and your spears. You're not going to have to fight and struggle and try to make things happen. You're coming into a season of ease." Instead of a sword you're going to need a plow to prepare the ground for the coming harvest. You can put your spear down. You're not going to have to attack and try to get back what belongs to you. God is fighting your battles. He's putting pressure on those who have what's yours. They're not going to be able to keep

> *You need to get ready for the harvest—not for a fight, not for a battle.*

it. You need to get ready for the harvest—not for a fight, not for a battle. Get ready for the breakthrough, get ready for healing. You're coming into an anointing of ease.

I have a friend who struggled with a drug addiction for many years. In high school, he got mixed up with the wrong crowd, and twenty years later he was still addicted. He had gone through counseling and treatment with no success. It looked as though that was his lot in life. Like the Israelites, he was defeated. The addiction was much bigger, and there was nothing he could do about it. But a couple of years ago, I ran into him. After being addicted for twenty-plus years, he was totally free. He looked better than he did in high school. His skin was clear, and he had regained his weight. He had a smile. I asked him how he did it. I thought he must have gone to a special program, gotten some kind of intensive treatment. He said, "No, Joel. I didn't do anything new. I can't really put my finger on it. It was just as though something broke inside. I suddenly felt a strength that I had never felt before." What was that? His cows came finding him. God gave him the victory, and he didn't have to fight. It was easier than he thought.

Freedom belongs to you. Wholeness belongs to you. Don't believe the lies that you're stuck, that you'll never get well, that it's too hard, that you've tried. This is a new day. That yoke of bondage is being broken, and you're getting a new yoke—a yoke of ease, a yoke of freedom, a yoke of victory. You're going to break habits that seemed permanent. It's not going to happen by your might, by your power. It's going to happen because the Most High God breathes on your life. It may have been difficult in the past. You've tried, and it didn't work out. Try again. You're in a new season. You're coming into harvest. You can put your sword down. You don't have to do it in your own strength. God is fighting that battle. Do your part and believe. Dare to declare, "I am free. I am whole. I am victorious." As with this man, God is going to

> *That yoke of bondage is being broken, and you're getting a new yoke—a yoke of ease, a yoke of freedom, a yoke of victory.*

surprise you. What you couldn't make happen, what you tried to do for years, suddenly you're going to see it turn around.

The Rough Places Made Smooth

Several years before my father died in 1999, we came across a construction permit to build the last full power television station in Houston. It was a big deal, and we were very excited. The transmitter was going to be located out of the city, but we needed a commercial building in town for the station as well as access to a telecommunication tower close by so we could send our microwave signal to the transmission site. Several months earlier, a man had called me out of the blue and left a message saying that he was in commercial real estate, and if we ever needed anything, he'd love to help. Normally, I would have deleted it as just another sales call, not thought much about it. But for some reason I wrote down his name and stuck it in my desk drawer, never dreaming that in a few months we'd need a building for the station. When I called him, it was as though we were old friends. He was very likable. He took us to different office buildings that were nice, but our challenge was to find one with a telecommunication tower close by. We looked for several weeks and couldn't find anything.

One day he took us to a big office complex on a hundred acres, very beautiful, with trees and lakes. There were new owners, and they were very excited at the possibility of having a television station. They said we would be their premier tenant and that they would give us the main sign out front. They showed us offices overlooking a lake. They wanted us so badly, and their price was almost half that of any property we'd seen. We loved the place. The only problem was that we had to find out how close a telecommunication tower was. We went on top of the building and looked around, but we didn't see any tower. I was disappointed, thinking this would have been perfect.

Everyone else left except Victoria and me. We stayed and walked around the property. As we were coming up the backside of the parking lot, about forty yards away I could hear heavy construction equipment on the other side of a wooden fence. I climbed up on it and looked over. The workers were pouring a foundation. I called out to one of the men and asked him what they were building, and he said, "A cell phone tower." I almost fell off the fence. I asked if there was room on it for other clients. He said, "Yes, it's brand new." I called the company, and the next day we had space to send our microwave signal to the transmitter. Everything had fallen into place.

> *All the "lucky breaks" you've been having are the hand of God.*

What was that? God making my life easier, going before me and making my rough places smooth. "Well, Joel, that's just a lucky break." No, all the "lucky breaks" you've been having are the hand of God. That's the yoke of ease. When you recognize His favor, when you take time to say, "Father, thank You for making my life easier. Thank You for Your goodness," then you will see more of His favor.

What's interesting is that when we were struggling to find property to build a new sanctuary and heard the news that the

> *God has the right people lined up for you, the right breaks, the solutions to problems.*

Compaq Center was coming available, one of the first people I called was this same realtor. He worked hand-in-hand with the city and was very instrumental in us getting this facility. What were the chances of that man calling me at the right time, or of me saving his number, or of him taking us to a place where a tower was being built? That's not random. That's not a coincidence. That was God causing the cows to find us. God is in control of your life. He knows what you need and how to get it to you. We all go through seasons of struggle, seasons of difficulty, but that's not your permanent home. You're coming into an anointing of ease. God has the right people lined up for you, the right breaks, the solutions to problems. He's directing your steps. As I did, you're going to see things fall into place. You're going to know it's the goodness of God.

A Yoke of Ease Is Coming

A friend of mine grew up very poor. His family lived in public housing. There was a lot of crime and drugs. His parents were migrant farmers and had no education. It looked as though this young man would never amount to much. His mother saw that he had a love for music, and she encouraged him to join the band in school. He became a top tuba player. In the sixth grade, he was already six foot six. He became the star on the basketball team and had thirty scholarship offers to play basketball when he graduated. He was headed to the Portland Trailblazers to play professional when he suffered a career-ending injury. He ended up back at home, without a good education and no money. He was working for the city as a dogcatcher, making a little more than minimum wage.

During my friend's lunch hour, he would go to the local music store and play the keyboards while wearing his dogcatcher uniform. Customers would gather around to listen to him play. They were mesmerized by his ability. One day a customer told the owner that she wanted to buy "the piano that the dogcatcher was playing." This happened again and again. The owner said to the young man, "These people aren't really buying my pianos. They're buying your sound. They love what you do." He offered him a full-time job to play the piano all day. That was the first step in his musical career. Today, my friend Ben Tankard has become known as the godfather of gospel jazz music. He's sold millions of albums, and he pastors a church. He travels the world sharing his gift of music.

Just as with Ben, God is working behind the scenes, lining up what you need. You're coming into a season when you're not going to have to fight. You're not going to have to struggle. You can put down your sword, because you're coming into a harvest season. You're going to see the goodness of God making your life easier. You may be in a difficult time, but God is about to take the pressure off. You're going to have a strength that you didn't have. People are going to go out of their way to be good to you. That yoke of bondage is coming off, and a yoke of ease is coming on. This is a new day. Things are turning in your favor. What's hindered you in the past is not going to hinder you anymore. Overcoming obstacles is going to be easier than you think. You're going to accomplish your dreams, and it's going to be easier than you think. As with the Israelites, you're not going to have to fight. The cows are going to find you. I believe and declare that ease is coming your way.

> *You can put down your sword, because you're coming into a harvest season.*

CHAPTER ELEVEN

Beautiful in Its Time

Solomon was the wisest man who ever lived. He wrote in the book of Ecclesiastes, "There is a time for everything: a time for joy and a time for sadness, a time to harvest and a time to plant, a time to be born and a time to die." He was saying that life is going to happen to us all. There are going to be different seasons, ups and downs, victories and losses, good friends and betrayals, promotions and setbacks. If he stopped there, we'd think, *Tell me something new.* We know all that, and it's kind of depressing. After listing all the things that can happen—the disappointments, the losses, the bad breaks—Solomon says, "I've thought about this and come to the conclusion that God makes all things beautiful in its time." He was saying, "You're going to go through things that are unfair. People will do you wrong. You'll have a setback in your health. A child will get off course. It's easy to live discouraged and think it's never going to work out. But if you just stay in faith and keep moving forward, in time God will make all things beautiful."

It may not be beautiful right now. Nothing's beautiful about going through a loss, dealing with an illness, or having a family member who won't speak to you. Just give it some time. You don't have to live worried and not be able to sleep at night. God is working behind the scenes. He's going to resolve things that look as though they could never be resolved. What you thought was going to limit you for the rest of your life—the bad break, the disappointment, the mistake you made—is not how your story ends. Beauty is coming, restoration is coming, healing is coming. It's going to turn out better than you've imagined.

God will make *all* things beautiful—not just the good breaks, not just the promotions, not just the divine connections. He'll make the disappointments, the losses, and the mistakes beautiful as well. That's how awesome our God is. Don't give up on your dreams. Don't live sour because of what didn't work out, bitter over the person who walked away, or upset over the contract that should have been yours. Let it go. God saw what happened. He has beauty for the ashes. He has joy for the morning. He says that He will pay you back double for the wrongs. He just needs some time. While you're waiting, stay in faith. That's when it's easy to get discouraged and say, "Why is this happening? When is it ever going to turn around? This is not fair." Pass the test. Keep doing the right thing. Keep going to work with a good attitude. Keep praising when you could be complaining. Keep speaking victory in the face of defeat. God is still on the throne. He has you in the

> *He'll make the disappointments, the losses, and the mistakes beautiful as well. That's how awesome our God is.*

palms of His hands. At the right time, you're going to see Him show out in your life in such a way that you won't think about what you lost. You'll be so blessed that you won't think about who did you wrong. You'll be so fulfilled that you won't dwell on the negative things in your past.

Just Give It Some Time

Maybe you grew up in dysfunction and didn't have a good childhood. You could accept that you're at a disadvantage, that you can't do anything great. But that didn't stop your destiny. You keep honoring God and He's going to make up for what you didn't get. He's going to open doors you couldn't open. He's going to have the right people come to you and help push you into your purpose. God saw what was unfair. He knows who left you out. He knows the times when you didn't think you could go on. He promises that He's going to make it beautiful. He's going to do something awesome in your life. Perhaps you went through a breakup, a divorce, and you're hurting, you're lonely. God is not finished. He's not going to leave you depressed and heartbroken. He has someone amazing coming, and you're going to be happier and more fulfilled than you've ever been. Don't judge the rest of your life by one difficult season. You may be in a time of struggle, a time of loss, a time when things aren't fair. Thoughts will tell you, *It's never going to change. This is your lot in life. Just accept it.* Don't believe those lies. God promises He will make all things beautiful. Now here's the key: Just give it some time.

> *Don't judge the rest of your life by one difficult season.*

We looked briefly at the Scripture, "The Israelites did not wait for God's plan to unfold." They missed out on going into the Promised Land because they got impatient and complained, thinking that God had forgotten about them. The mistake we often make is to get in a hurry when we don't think it's going to happen. Voices whisper, "If it was going to happen, it would have happened by now." Trust the process. God makes everything beautiful in its time. Give Him time to work it out. If it hasn't happened yet, it hasn't been the right time. When God is ready, all the forces of darkness cannot stop Him. When it's your time to see beauty, promotion, and vindication, it will happen. People don't determine your destiny. Bad breaks, disappointments, and even mistakes you've made don't cancel what God has ordained for you. God has taken that all into account.

How we wait is important. We can't wait upset and discouraged, saying, "God, why did this happen? Why did these people do me wrong?" That's going to delay the beauty. The right way to wait is in an attitude of faith, knowing that God is on the throne, knowing that He's working all things for your good, expecting His favor, and declaring His promises. It's saying, "This difficulty didn't come to stay; it came to pass. God being for me is more than the world being against me." While you're waiting, be good to others. Be a blessing to your friends and encourage your coworkers. While you're waiting for your child to get back on course, go help another young person get back on course. While you're waiting for the promotion, help someone else rise higher. While you're waiting for healing, pray for someone else who needs healing. When we've been through loss, hurts, and disappointments, it's easy to sit around nursing our wounds, thinking about what we've been through and how unfair it was. Do yourself a favor and get your mind off yourself and go out and be a blessing. As you help others, God is going to help you.

> *The right way to wait is in an attitude of faith, knowing that God is on the throne, knowing that He's working all things for your good, expecting His favor, and declaring His promises.*

Everything Serves His Plan

The Scripture says, "Everything serves His plan." It's not just the good breaks and the promotions that serve His plan. The disappointments, the closed doors, and the people who did you wrong are serving His plan. Without that happening you couldn't reach your destiny. You have to trust the process. God's ways are not our ways. We see the bad breaks or the person who left us out as negative, but the truth is that all these are necessary to become who we were created to be.

A friend of mine started a new business. He and his wife worked tirelessly, year after year, pouring their hearts and souls into it. I would call him in the evening and he would be out meeting with clients several nights a week. They saw some success. It was profitable, but then they hit a limit that they couldn't seem to get past. At one point, the owner of the building where my friend leased space for his company converted the parking lot into a big parking garage. Now his customers had to park off-site and take a shuttle. It seemed as though the harder he worked, the worse it got. His dream was to leave the company to his children as a legacy of success, but after thirty years they had to close the doors. He was so disappointed. He told me he felt like a failure. He was embarrassed, ashamed, and hurt. He thought, *God, how could You let this happen to me? I gave it my best. I have nothing to show for all these years of hard work.* For three years he was not himself. He had been so positive, so full of faith, but when I would call, he didn't have any passion. He'd lost his fire. We all go through things that don't make sense, but God wouldn't allow it if it wasn't going to serve His plan. This is when you have to dig down deep and say, "God, I don't understand this, but I trust You. I believe that You're still ordering my steps and that You still have good things in store for me."

One day a door unexpectedly opened for my friend to a position where he could use his gifts in a much greater way. He was so excited. He said, "I feel as though the thirty years I put into my former business were not lost, but they were to prepare me for what I'm doing now." He calls his new job "the position of a lifetime." The number of people he used to impact in a year, he now impacts in a day. God knows how to make all things beautiful if you just give Him the time. If you have some things that you're disappointed about, that you don't understand, that were unfair, just keep moving forward. God is not going to waste anything you went through. It feels like a setback, but it's really a setup. You're about to come out to new levels. You're going to go places that you've never gone and see favor that you've never seen. Quit believing the lie that you've had too many bad breaks. "God must have forgotten about you. You have a good reason to live sour. Look at what you've been through." That was all setting you up for something you've never imagined. I believe even now you're about to step into some of this beauty. The things that were meant to harm you, the struggles that have tried to discourage you, the people who did you

> *God is not going to waste anything you went through.*

wrong, the bad breaks that should have limited your life—God is turning it all to your advantage. This is a new day. God is doing a new thing. You're about to see vindication, restoration, new opportunities, and divine connections. The tide is turning in your favor.

The Potter Never Takes His Hands Off

There's a couple who attend Lakewood and who are very faithful. They raised their son here, but when he went off to college, he started running with the wrong crowd, partying, making poor choices. One thing led to another, and he ended up with a drug addiction. His parents tried to help him, but he didn't want to have anything to do with them. He got to the point where he wouldn't speak to them or have any contact with them. It was breaking their hearts. They would come for prayer week after week. They couldn't understand it. They had done the right thing, but the wrong thing happened. They could have been bitter and complained, "God, where are You?" But they just kept doing the right thing, being faithful, serving, giving, helping others.

The Scripture says, "God is the potter, and we are the clay." There's nothing beautiful about clay. It's just an earthy material that develops plasticity when wet. But the potter puts the clay on the wheel and begins to spin it around and around. While it's spinning, the clay is wobbly, still has lumps, and doesn't look like much, but the potter never takes his hands off the clay. He keeps molding it until it begins to take the shape of a vase or plate or bowl. If someone came up to the potter and saw the clay going around, they might say, "You're wasting your time. That's just a lump of worthless clay. That's never going to amount to much." The potter would reply, "Just give me some time. You see clay and think it's a bunch of dirt, but I see something beautiful. I see a valuable vase."

This young man was off course, making poor decisions, but God is the potter. He never takes His hands off the clay. Even though it's wobbly, even though it has lumps, even though it falls down and He has to reshape it, He keeps working. All those times when you thought God had forgotten about you, the truth is that God still had His hands on you. When you weren't making good decisions, when you were running with the wrong crowd and giving in to temptations, He didn't throw you out because you're clay, because He found some lumps, because you have faults and weak-

> *All those times when you thought God had forgotten about you, the truth is that God still had His hands on you.*

nesses. His hands have always been on you, and the good news is that He's never going to take His hands off you. The Scripture says, "His calling on your life is irrevocable." He's going to keep making you and molding you. In the same way, the potter's hands are on your children. They may get off course, but the potter doesn't give up on the clay. He just spins it around a little bit more.

These parents understood what Solomon says, that there's a time for weeping, a time for loss, a time for disappointment, but that's not the end of the story. God also says He will make all things beautiful in its time. There's a time for restoration, a time for healing, a time for deliverance, a time for celebration. Their attitude was: *God, we don't understand it, but we trust You. We know that You're in control. We know that You won't take Your hands off our son. We know that You will keep making him and molding him.* After thirteen years of their son barely speaking to them, one day he called and said he wanted to come home and make things right. He came back to church and went to treatment. He's been free for six years now. Today, he's helping other young people get free. If you stay in faith, and you give God the time, He'll make all things beautiful.

As with this couple, you may have relationships that are strained. You may have family members who won't have anything to do with you. You think it's always going to be this way. You're about to write them off. No, keep loving them, keep being good to them, keep praying, keep forgiving, and stay on the high road. God sees what's happening. He knows how to restore. He knows how to change people's hearts. His hands are still on them. They may need to go around the wheel a few more times. The timing is not up to us; it's up to God. Will you wait for His plan to unfold? Will you not get discouraged and say, "When is it going to happen? Why isn't it improving?"

It just needs some time. When you understand this principle, it takes the pressure off. You won't live frustrated, wondering how it's going to work out. You'll say, "God, everything is not perfect in my life. I'm

> *The timing is not up to us; it's up to God. Will you wait for His plan to unfold?*

waiting for things to change, but I'm going to enjoy today, knowing that You're on the throne and at the right time You're going to make all things beautiful in my life."

Bitter to Sweet

In Exodus 15, Moses was leading the Israelites through the desert to the Promised Land. The people were so hot and thirsty that they didn't think they were going to make it. They desperately needed water. They finally came to a pool of water at a place called Marah and were so excited that they rushed to it, but the water was bitter. They couldn't drink it. Their excitement turned to great disappointment. God showed Moses a certain kind of tree, and when he cast it into the bitter water, the waters were made sweet. Now the people could drink all the water they wanted. God knows how to take a bitter situation—a bitter loss, a bitter breakup, a bitter childhood—and make it sweet. It looks as though that bitterness is your destiny, that you just need to learn to live with it. In the natural that would be true, but God is supernatural. That water may be bitter, but when God touches it, the bitterness will turn sweet. The relationship will be restored, the child will come home, the dream will come to pass.

The Scripture says, "After the Israelites left Marah, where the water was bitter, they came to Elim, where there were twelve springs and seventy palm trees, and they camped near the water." They came out of the bitterness into an oasis. It was like a resort. I can imagine them thinking, *How did this beautiful place ever make it into the desert?* The principle is that God is going to bring you out of the bitter places of life, not just to where you were, but to an oasis, to an abundance, joy, health, and fulfillment like you've never seen. It's going to be a time of refreshing, reenergizing, and enjoyment that you've never experienced. When God makes all things beautiful, it's going to exceed your expectations. Your relationships will be healthier than ever, and your children will be doing awesome things. You'll be going further in your career, stepping into new levels of your destiny. From bitter waters to sweet waters, from the desert to an oasis—that's how God restores. That's His idea of beauty.

> God is going to bring you out of the bitter places of life, not just to where you were, but to an oasis, to an abundance, joy, health, and fulfillment like you've never seen.

Second Chances

In Acts 13, the apostle Paul chose Barnabas and his cousin John Mark to travel with him on his first missionary journey. Paul could have chosen anyone. He was very influential and very respected. They went to different cities ministering and were having great success. But when Paul decided to sail to the city of Perga, the Scripture says that "John Mark deserted them." It doesn't give any reason for why he went back home to Jerusalem. But Paul was upset. He thought, *At least you could have told me you were going to leave. After all, I chose you, took you under my wing, shared my influence, and now you just walk away.* Later, when Paul and Barnabas were about to return to check on how the new believers were doing in the cities where they had been, Barnabas wanted to take John Mark with them. But Paul disagreed strongly, saying in effect, "No way. He's not coming back on the team. He deserted us before. He'll just quit on us again when the going gets tough." It led to such a sharp disagreement that Paul and Barnabas split up. They were so at odds that they no longer traveled together. Paul chose Silas and Barnabas chose John Mark, and they went their separate ways.

You don't read much more about Barnabas and John Mark. But Paul and Silas did great things on this second missionary journey, saw one miracle after another. When they were in the Philippian prison, at midnight they sang praises and the prison doors were opened. Much later, when Paul was on his way to stand trial in Rome, he was shipwrecked on the island of Malta and a poisonous snake bit him on the hand. Paul just shook it off, and it didn't harm him. After Paul prayed for the father of the chief man of the island and he was healed, all the sick people on the island came and were healed. There is chapter after chapter of how God used

Paul, and how he went on to write almost half the books in the New Testament.

I can imagine that John Mark thought, *Man, I blew it. Why didn't I stick with Paul? Why did I desert him? At least I should have thanked him for choosing me and told him that I wanted to go home. I shouldn't have just disappeared.* It seemed as though his own mistakes, his own poor choices, had soured this relationship and limited his destiny. We can all look back as John Mark did and think, *Man, if I had only stayed in that relationship, or if I'd only been more committed in my marriage, or if I'd only spent more time with my children, or if I'd only finished college, where could I be now?* But God has a way of making all things beautiful, even the mistakes we've made, even our own shortcomings, things we know we should have done better.

> God has a way of making all things beautiful, even the mistakes we've made, even our own shortcomings, things we know we should have done better.

John Mark was down on himself. When he heard how great Paul was doing and how he was impacting cities, it must have felt like pouring salt on a wound. He thought, *That could have been me.* Fast forward many years later. Paul is now an old man. He's in prison for the faith and about to pass. He's writing to Timothy and says, "I've fought the good fight, I've finished the race, I've kept the faith." He goes on to say, "Timothy, when you come, bring the coat I left in Troas, bring my books and papers. And one more thing, bring John Mark with you, for he is very profitable to me." Of all the things Paul could have asked for at the end of his life, he asked for John Mark. I can imagine word getting to John Mark from Timothy: "You're not going to believe this, but Paul is asking for you. He wants me to bring you." John Mark probably replied,

"Don't kid me like that. You know I blew it with Paul." Timothy would answer, "No, I'm not kidding. Paul wants you to come. He said that you are very valuable to him." I can see tears welling up in John Mark's eyes.

It's Not Too Late for the Beautiful

It's impossible to say what changed with Paul. He hadn't wanted to have anything to do with John Mark. He'd lost all trust in him, but God knows how to soften people's hearts. He knows how to give you another chance. In His time, He will make all things beautiful. You may have relationships that you think are too far gone, that there's too much water under the bridge. You messed up, and they're not going to have anything to do with you. No, another chance is coming. You wouldn't be reading this if God wasn't about to do something unusual, something out of the ordinary. John Mark thought he'd missed his chance, that his bad choices stopped his purpose. But here's how good God is. John Mark not only saw his relationship with Paul restored, but most scholars believe that he wrote the Gospel of Mark. Who would have ever

> *Who would have ever thought that after deserting Paul, after causing a disagreement that caused Barnabas to break away from Paul, that today we'd be reading the book that John Mark wrote?*

thought that after deserting Paul, after causing a disagreement that caused Barnabas to break away from Paul, that today we'd be reading the book that John Mark wrote? What am I saying? God knows how to make all things beautiful. Just give it some time.

"Well, Joel, this is encouraging, but I think it's too late for me. You don't know what I've done, the relationships that I've soured, and the regrets that I have." Your mistakes are not too much for the mercy of God. Your shortcomings, your failures, and your lack of commitment did not stop your destiny. God is softening hearts right now. He's preparing the way for restoration. Timothy sent word, "Go find John Mark and tell him that Paul says he's profitable, that he's valuable, that he needs him." God is calling your name today. "Go find Linda, go find Phillip, go find Rolando. Tell them that they're valuable, that they have another chance, that I'm going to restore what was stolen." It's not too late. You haven't made too many mistakes. As with John Mark, your latter days are going to be better than your former days. Mistakes you've made in the past are not going to keep you from the great things God has in store.

Maybe you're not John Mark in this story, though. Perhaps you're Paul. God is saying, "Give them another chance. Show mercy." It's time to forgive. It's time to release the hurt. It's time to bury the hatchet. This is a new day. As you forgive, God is going to make things beautiful in your life. You're not just doing them a favor; you're doing yourself a favor. Make that call and tell your child, your parent, or your friend that you need them. Tell them that they're valuable to you. God didn't put them in your life by accident. The mercy you show them is the mercy that's going to be shown to you. Life is flying by, and time is short. They're not always going to be here. Paul waited until he was almost done. But he couldn't really say "I have finished my course," without saying, "Go get John Mark." He was saying, "I'm not going to die with anything between him and me. I'm not going to die with him thinking that

> *As you forgive, God is going to make things beautiful in your life.*

I'm disappointed in him, feeling guilty and condemned. I'm bigger than that. It's time to give him another chance." When John Mark came and felt Paul's love and acceptance, gifts that had been buried in him came alive. Vision that lay dormant came back to life. He stepped up, wrote his book, and saw God's favor in new ways.

I believe God is about to make some things beautiful in your life today. Whether you made the mistakes as John Mark did or life threw you some curves, some bad breaks, some disappointments that are not your fault, God saw it. Your time is coming. He didn't bring you this far to leave you. Things that look as though they'll never work out in your health, your relationships, or your career, just give it some time. God is still on the throne. He's working behind the scenes. Now do your part. Instead of living discouraged, all through the day you have to say, "Father, thank You that You're making all things beautiful in my life." If you do this, I believe and declare that things are about to happen that you couldn't make happen. As John Mark did, you're going to see restoration, and you're going to accomplish dreams bigger than you thought. It's going to be more beautiful than you can imagine.

CHAPTER TWELVE

Manasseh Is Coming

We all go through things that are unfair, through situations that cause heartache and pain. We were doing the right thing, but somebody walked away, or we came down with an illness, or our child got off course. It's easy to get discouraged and think that's our lot in life, that everyone lives with disappointments. But if you stay in faith and don't get bitter, God is going to bless you in such a way that you don't remember the pain of the past. Yes, you went through difficulties, things you don't understand, but now you're so blessed, so fulfilled, so happy that you don't dwell on who hurt you, what didn't work out, or how you weren't raised in a healthy environment. You may not totally forget it, but it's not on the top of your mind as it used to be. You don't wake up thinking about it, and you don't go through the day sour. You're too blessed to be angry, too blessed to be bitter, too blessed to hold a grudge, and too blessed to think about what didn't work out.

"Causing You to Forget" Is Coming

This is what happened with Joseph. He had a lot of unfair things happen to him. He was betrayed by his brothers, thrown into a pit, and eventually sold into slavery. It's one thing for people to be against you, but this was his own brothers, the people who should have loved him. That made it much more painful. As a slave, he was falsely accused of a crime by the master's wife and put in prison for several years. Then one day he interpreted a dream for Pharaoh, who was so impressed that he put Joseph in charge of all of Egypt. Joseph ended up bringing his whole family to Egypt, including the brothers who threw him into the pit. He gave them a place to live and provided them land to grow their crops.

One day Joseph and his wife had a baby. The Scripture says, "Joseph named his first son Manasseh. 'For,' he said, 'the Lord has caused me to forget all my troubles and the pain of my past.'"

> *Joseph had been through all kinds of hardships, betrayals, injustice, and lonely nights, but now God had blessed him in such a way that he didn't think about the heartache he'd been through.*

Joseph had been through all kinds of hardships, betrayals, injustice, and lonely nights, but now God had blessed him in such a way that he didn't think about the heartache he'd been through. He was so fulfilled, so grateful, that he didn't live bitter because of his brothers or upset because he'd spent years in prison. He was so blessed, so favored, that he didn't have time to be angry or to try to pay people back. He was too overwhelmed with the goodness of God. As with Joseph, you may have had things come against you that weren't fair. Perhaps you did your best but a dream didn't work out, or your marriage didn't make it, or you lost a loved one. It was painful. Thoughts whisper, *It's never going to change. This is as good as it gets. Just learn to live with it.* No, get ready. Manasseh, which means "causing to forget," is coming. God is going to cause you to forget. He's going to bless you in such a way that you don't remember the pain of the past. It's not going to be on the forefront of your mind. You're going to be so filled with gratitude for all God has done that you won't think about what you've been through.

We talk a lot about letting go of the past, forgiving the people who hurt us, and not reliving disappointments. That's important. But sometimes it's hard to not think about what went wrong. You wake up, and the heartache comes to mind. Through the day, you want to be happy but you feel the heaviness reminding you of the loss, the sickness you're dealing with, or the addiction. We try to tune it out, but it's an ongoing struggle. There will be a day when God is going to cause you to forget. You're going to give birth to Manasseh. God is going to make up for it in such an amazing way that you're not going to remember the pain of the past. You're not going to wake up thinking about who hurt you. You're going to wake up thinking about how blessed you are. You're not going to go through the day feeling discouraged by the loss and carrying the heaviness. God

> *There will be a day when God is going to cause you to forget.*

is going to turn things around to where all you can think about is how grateful you are. You're going to have a deep satisfaction, a joy, that you can't explain. What happened? You gave birth to Manasseh.

Dealing with the Pain of the Past

"Well, Joel, I've been through a lot of difficulties. I still remember the heartache, the loss, the sickness. That hasn't happened for me." Don't get discouraged. You may not realize it, but you're pregnant, so to speak. Your Manasseh is coming. God hasn't forgotten about you. He's seen the heartache, the lonely nights, and the injustice. God has collected every tear you've shed. You may not be able to forget on your own, but the good news is that God is going to cause you to forget. He's going to turn it around in such a way that you're overwhelmed. You won't have time to think about the hurt because you're so grateful for the goodness of God.

When my father went to be with the Lord, it was painful. I was so close to him, and he was taken sooner than I wanted. But as with Joseph, God has blessed me in such a way that I don't remember the pain. He's brought gifts out of me that I hadn't known I had. He's given me ability, influence, and favor that I never had. Yes, I miss my father, I don't forget him, and I honor his legacy. But God has caused me to forget the pain of the past.

If God had only delivered Joseph from slavery and the prison, that would be justice. But God had Joseph's brothers come before him and apologize. They were at Joseph's mercy. God always does more than we can ask or think of. God put Joseph in charge of the nation. He was blessed with resources, land, and opportunity. He had influence and favor, and his children were blessed. God didn't just bring Joseph out, He brought him out in an exceptional way. We all have things we need to forget—a bad break, a mistake we

> *Your mind will be so full of God's goodness that the negative memory doesn't have any space to come up.*

made, a door that closed and caused heartache. When it comes up, try your best to let it go and don't dwell on it, but at some point God is going to do something out of the ordinary that will cause you to forget it. You won't have to struggle with it in your thoughts. Your mind will be so full of God's goodness that the negative memory doesn't have any space to come up.

Sometimes people tell me, "Joel, I'm praying for you. I know you have people who come against you, people who don't like you." I appreciate them praying, and I know they mean well. But God has been so good to me, He's honored and blessed me in such a way, I don't even think about the negative. My mind is so overwhelmed with gratitude, with thanksgiving, that God has caused me to forget. When I drive up to what was called the Compaq Center, and I think that this is where I used to have season tickets to watch basketball games and now it's our church, I'm still amazed. Sometimes I'm flipping through television channels and I come across programs where I'm speaking and I think, *How did I get there?* I gave birth to Manasseh. Yes, there have been difficult times—losing my father was hard, people have tried to stop us—but I'm too blessed to be bitter, to be stressed out, or to be offended. When I think about the goodness of God and where He's brought me, how He's opened doors that I couldn't open and caused the right people to be good to me, I don't have time to think about the troubles and pain in the past. I don't have time to try to pay people back. God has been too good to me. He's caused me to forget.

Joy That Will Go On Forever

God says in Isaiah 61, "Because you got a double dose of trouble, your inheritance in the land will be doubled and your joy will go on forever." God doesn't promise that we won't have trouble. Sometimes we'll have a double dose of trouble, more than our fair share. But the good news is that trouble doesn't have the final say.

> *God promises that He won't just help you get through it, help you survive it, but He'll bring you out with double—double the joy, double the strength, double the influence, double the resources.*

The betrayal, the sickness, or the loss is not how your story ends. God promises that He won't just help you get through it, help you survive it, but He'll bring you out with double—double the joy, double the strength, double the influence, double the resources. God makes the enemy pay for bringing the trouble. God says your joy will go on forever. That means the trouble is not permanent, the pain is not permanent. That means the loneliness, the addiction, or the depression is not going to last. God says restoration is coming, new beginnings are coming, abundance, victory, and breakthroughs are coming. The pain is only temporary; the joy will go on forever.

You may have been through a lot of pain in the past. Maybe you have things coming against you now, and it doesn't seem as though it will ever change. Get ready. Manasseh is coming. God has something ahead of you that will cause you to be so blessed, so fulfilled, so prosperous, that you'll live out of a place of joy and gratefulness. You'll think, *God, You've amazed me with Your goodness. You've done more than I ever dreamed.* You won't wake up thinking about the haters; you'll wake up thinking about the goodness of God. You won't go through the day bitter because of bad breaks; you'll go through saying, "Lord, thank You for Your favor. Thank You for what You've done." You won't go to bed discouraged, dwelling on what you didn't get, sour over what didn't work out. You will lie down in peace, overwhelmed with gratitude, thinking about the greatness of our God.

I talked to a lady who's well known. She was raised in poverty and didn't have a good childhood. Many times she and her siblings didn't have food. Her father wasn't in her life. She was taken advantage of by men. There was a lot of hurt, pain, and abuse. Her mother took her to church each week. As a little girl, going through years of heartache and things she didn't understand, she would tell people, "Jesus is my daddy." Against all odds, God opened doors for her and caused people to show her favor and made things happen that she couldn't make happen. Today, she's one of the most influential people in the world. Every time she walks through her house and looks out and sees the ocean, under her breath she says, "Thank You, Jesus." Dozens of times a day, she thanks God for His goodness. She had a rough start, she was abused, and life wasn't fair. But as Joseph did, she gave birth to Manasseh. God blessed her in such a great way that He caused her to forget.

You may not have had to deal with anything that difficult, but we've all had things that could steal our joy and cause us to lose our passion and settle for mediocrity. But God is saying to you, "Manasseh is coming." There's something in your future that's going to erase the pain of the past. God is not going to just bring you out. He's not going to just vindicate you, restore you, and heal you. That would be good, but that wouldn't make you forget the pain. God is going to do something out of the ordinary, something unusual, something that you don't see com-

> *There's something in your future that's going to erase the pain of the past.*

ing. When Manasseh shows up, you're going to say, "Wow, God! I never dreamed this would happen. I never dreamed I would be this blessed. I never dreamed we'd be in the Compaq Center. I never dreamed I'd meet a spouse this great. I never dreamed I'd be this happy."

Something Amazing Is in Front of You

A friend of mine was married for over twenty years. One day he came home from a business trip and found a note from his wife on the kitchen table saying she was leaving. She had found another man, and their marriage was over. He was devastated. He loved his wife. For several years he tried to convince her to change her mind.

> *When you go through a bad break, through an injustice, you become pregnant, so to speak. Manasseh is conceived in your spirit.*

He stood in faith and prayed and believed, but she never did. At one point he finally realized it was over. He didn't understand it. It didn't seem fair. But I've learned not to put a question mark where God puts a period. We're not going to understand everything that happens. Life is not always fair. You can't make people do what's right. God has given us our own free will. Sometimes people make choices that hurt us. What the brothers did to Joseph wasn't fair. He hadn't done them any wrong. But God is a God of justice. He doesn't just heal the hurts. That would be good enough. We would be grateful just to be restored. But God is so amazing that He's going to cause you to forget the pain of the past. When you go through a bad break, through an injustice, you become pregnant, so to speak. Manasseh is conceived in your spirit.

You may have been through unfair situations, not treated right growing up, betrayed by a friend. You may be taking a treatment to try to beat an illness. Life has thrown you a curve. The good news is, you're pregnant. There's a baby coming, something out of the ordinary, an explosive blessing, a divine connection, a supernatural opportunity. You couldn't have made it happen, and you weren't next in line. What was it? Manasseh. It is God blessing you in such a way that causes you to forget the hurt, forget the injustice, forget what you've been through.

This friend of mine had been so outgoing, so fun to be around, but after his wife left, he lost his passion. I told him what I'm telling you: "That is not how your story ends. God is not only going to bring you through, but He's going to do something to make up for it." About a year later, he met a beautiful lady. When I saw him with her, he was beaming with joy. They fell in love and got married. He said, "Joel, I have never been this happy in all my life. I didn't know what true love is." What was that? He gave birth to Manasseh. God knows how to cause you to forget the pain of the past.

Somebody may have walked out on you. That's not easy, and the hurt is real, but it's not the end. God has the final say. He's going to bring you somebody so great, so fun, so talented, so good-looking, so well off that you're not going to miss the person who left you. Manasseh is coming. God is going to pay you back. Now get your hopes up. Quit believing the lies that say, "You've seen your best days. You'll never be happy. You've been through too much." God has something amazing in front of you—amazing people, amazing opportunities, amazing influence, amazing resources. He has something that you've never seen. He has something more rewarding, more fulfilling than you've ever dreamed.

> *He has something more rewarding, more fulfilling than you've ever dreamed.*

A Double of Favor

I love that the Scripture says that God will cause you to forget. Sometimes we can't forget on our own. When we've had something happen that really hurts—we lost a loved one, a person walked out of a relationship, an unexpected illness—we can do our best to let it go and move forward, but the thoughts keep coming. *It wasn't fair. You're a victim. It's never going to get better.* We can't totally forget on our own, but God will bless you in such a way that He causes you to forget.

In Chapter Seven, I mentioned that Ruth was a young lady in the Scripture who lost her husband. She was devastated, now a widow. Her dreams were shattered. She couldn't forget that. I can imagine every morning when she woke up, the thoughts came, saying, *Too bad that you're a victim. Life hasn't treated you fairly. Now you're stuck in poverty. Just learn to live with it.* A while later, when Ruth was out in the harvest field gathering the wheat the workers had missed, minding her own business, the Scripture says that God caused the owner of the field, a man named Boaz, to "notice her." God caused him to notice her. You may have gone through an unfair situation that you don't think will ever turn around, but you don't know who God is causing to notice you. Right now God is causing you to stand out, causing you to look good. A dozen people may overlook you, but God will cause that one

> *God will cause people to see you the way He wants them to see you.*

person to say, "Now, she's fine or he's amazing." God will cause people to see you the way He wants them to see you. When I walked into a jewelry store and met Victoria for the first time,

God caused her to see me as tall, dark, and handsome. We got married, and she found out none of that was true. Right now, God is causing the right people to be attracted to you. He's causing opportunities to find you, causing good breaks to chase you down.

Ruth had been through all this heartache, and she thought she'd seen her best days. But God caused Boaz, the wealthiest man in that area, to notice her. They ended up getting married and having a son. She never dreamed she'd be that blessed, never dreamed she'd be that well off, never dreamed she'd have children. Now, when she woke up each morning, the thoughts that told her she was a victim, that she'd been through too much, and that she'd never be happy didn't come anymore. God blessed her in such a great way that she forgot the pain of her past. God has some blessings coming your way that are going to cause you to forget what you've been through, forget who hurt you, forget what you lost, forget what wasn't fair. Get ready to give birth to Manasseh. You may have gotten a double dose of trouble, but a double dose of favor is coming.

"After This"

This is what happened with Job in the Scripture. Everything was going great, then the bottom fell out. He lost his business, his seven sons and three daughters, and his health. He had boils all over his body. It was very painful. What's interesting is that Job was a good man. The Scripture says, "Job loved God and lived with integrity." Just because we honor God doesn't mean we're not going to have difficulties and things we don't understand. What

Job couldn't see was that God allowed the difficulty. Satan had to ask for permission to test Job, and God only allowed him to test Job to a certain point. When you go through difficulties, you have to remind yourself that God is still in control. The person who did you wrong, the illness that set you back, or the relationship that didn't work out was not a surprise to God. Don't get bitter. Don't start complaining. It's a test.

> *When you go through difficulties, you have to remind yourself that God is still in control.*

Job didn't see how he could ever be happy again. Negative thoughts bombarded his mind, and he made the mistake of believing some of them. He said, "I will never see pleasure again." He was saying, "I've been through too much. I've seen my best days." He was so discouraged that a few verses later he said, "I hate my life." He didn't want to go on living. What's interesting is that even though Job had given up, even though he was complaining and cursing his future, God hadn't given up. God still had a plan. Job didn't realize that he was pregnant. When God allowed him to be tested, when He allowed the bad breaks, at the same time God planted a seed in Job. He conceived Manasseh.

Things kept getting worse. Job later said, "My eyes are dim from weeping, and I am but a shadow of my former self." Maybe as Job did, you feel like a shadow of what you used to be. At one time you were healthy and strong, full of energy, but now you're fighting an illness, dealing with the pain. You feel weak and tired. Or at one time you were blessed in your business, successful and had more than enough, but now things have gone down and you're struggling, barely making it. Or at one time you were happy, had a great marriage, and were excited about life, but things have changed. You're just going through the motions, trying to keep it together. It may not look good, but what you can't see is that Manasseh is coming. Being half of who you were is not how your story ends. The writer of Proverbs says, "The path of the righteous gets brighter and brighter," not darker and darker. The good news is, your water is about to break. It's not long before you give birth. God is not just

> *Being half of who you were is not how your story ends.*

going to do something that will restore you and get you back to where you were. He's going to bless you in such a way that you forget what you've been through.

Job thought his life was over. He didn't understand why he was suffering. He was negative and complaining. It seems to go on and on, but some Bible commentators say that the whole trial may have only lasted nine months. That's the same amount of time that a woman is pregnant. Nine months later, God turned it around and brought Job out with twice what he had before. Just as Isaiah said, Job got a double dose of trouble, so God gave him a double blessing. He had twice the sheep, twice the cattle, and twice the joy. The Scripture says in the final chapter of Job, "After this, Job lived a hundred and forty years and saw his grandchildren down to four generations." After what? After the heartache, after the loss, after the sickness. After the trouble and pain, you're going to see years of health, happiness, and favor, to where you

> *After the trouble and pain, you're going to see years of health, happiness, and favor, to where you don't look back and dwell on what you've been through.*

don't look back and dwell on what you've been through. I can hear Job saying, "What was I thinking, saying my life was over? Look what God has done. I'm seeing my great, great, great grandchildren." He was so happy and so fulfilled that he didn't think about what he'd been through.

You're About to Give Birth

What happened in Job's life also happened in Joseph's life. It was thirteen years from the time he was betrayed by his brothers to the time Pharaoh put him in charge of Egypt. Those in between years were very difficult, but after Joseph took the throne at the age of thirty, you don't read anything about him having problems, armies coming against him, or people betraying him. The difficulty was for a season. Joseph's son Manasseh had children, and Manasseh's children had children, and those children had children. After the betrayal, after being falsely accused, after going to prison unfairly, Joseph lived to see three generations in peace, in stability, in favor, in abundance. He was so grateful, so blessed, that he didn't think about his brothers betraying him. Every time he saw his son Manasseh, he'd say, "Father, thank You for being so good to me."

God says He will restore double and your joy will go on forever. The difficulties are temporary; the joy is permanent. You may be in a tough time, but get ready. Manasseh is coming. God has something in your future that's going to cause you to forget what you've been through. It was painful, and you may not be able to forget it on your own, but don't worry. God is going to cause you to forget. Right now He's working behind the scenes. You may not see any sign of it, but I assure you that you're pregnant. You're about to give birth to blessings that are going to catapult you ahead. God is going to do something unusual, something out of the ordinary, to make up for what you've been through. As with Ruth, the loss is not the end, and the right people are going to notice you. As with Job, the bad breaks are not your destiny, and double is coming. As with Joseph, the years of heartache are not your final chapter. I believe and declare that you are coming into years of health, happiness, growth, peace, favor, good relationships, and good breaks. God is going to cause you to forget the pain of the past.

CHAPTER THIRTEEN

Coming Out Better

Many times when we go through disappointments and things we don't understand, we're just grateful that we made it through. It's one thing to come through a difficulty beat up and bedraggled, looking worn and tired. But when God restores you, you're not going to look like what you've been through. Nobody is going to be able to tell that you went through the sickness, through the divorce, or through the unfair childhood. He's going to bring you back to your original condition, back to who you were created to be before the heartache, before the bad break. Some people make it out, but they age ten years in the process. The challenge takes so much out of them that they look run-down and tired. That's not you. God is not just going to bring you through; He's going to bring you out better, refreshed, renewed, and reenergized. Nobody will know what you've been through.

I met a young lady who was visiting our church with her husband and children. She's a very sharp woman. She handed me her book that is titled *Beauty for Ashes*. I asked what it was about, and she said it was her life story. I thought, *You're only in your twenties. What kind of story can you have?* She told how as a little girl her parents were on drugs and abandoned her, left her on the street.

She was passed from foster home to foster home and went through abuse and rejection, all kinds of unfair things. When I looked at her, what she was saying didn't match who I was seeing. I should have seen someone who was battle-scarred, run-down, insecure, and struggling. Instead, I saw someone who is beautiful, confident, strong, and well-spoken. I never dreamed she could have gone through that. I thought she'd come from a loving family and had a healthy childhood, but it was just the opposite. All the odds were against her, but she had her college degree, two beautiful children, a loving husband, and a successful career. That's the way God restores. He brings you through with no sign of the difficulty, no sign of the betrayal, no sign of the loss.

You may be in a challenging time now. Maybe it feels as though it's taken something out of you that can't be replaced. You've lost the spring in your step. You've accepted that you'll always be at a disadvantage. Get ready. God is about to breathe new life into your spirit. He's going to renew your strength and renew your youth like the eagle's. What that challenge took out, God is about to put back in—health, vitality, freshness, passion. He's going to bring new opportunities, good breaks, the right people, and favor that catapults you ahead. He's not going to just bring you out; He's going to make up for what was unfair. It's just as we read in the previous chapter that God says, "Because you got a double dose of trouble, your inheritance in the land will be double and your joy will go on forever." When you come into double, nobody will know that a business partner cheated you, nobody will know you had an unfair childhood, nobody will know you went through that illness. You're going to be so blessed, so healthy, so strong, and so favored that nobody will know what you've been through.

> *What that challenge took out, God is about to put back in—health, vitality, freshness, passion.*

Without the Smell of Smoke

In the book of Daniel, three Hebrew teenagers wouldn't bow down to King Nebuchadnezzar's golden idol. He was so upset that he had them thrown into a fiery furnace. They should have been killed instantly, but the Scripture says, "Not a hair on their heads was singed, their clothing was not scorched, and they didn't even smell like smoke." They came out with no sign that they had been in the fire. We would rejoice if they had just come out alive, battered, bruised, hair burned, and eyebrows singed. Just the fact that they survived would be a great miracle. But notice how God works. When He restores, there's no sign of trouble, no sign of fire, no sign of injustice, no sign of the bad break. God went so far as to not even have them smell like smoke. It's one thing to not see any sign of a fire, to not look like what you've been through, but God is so amazing that when He restores, you're not even going to smell like what you've been through.

> *When He restores, there's no sign of trouble, no sign of fire, no sign of injustice, no sign of the bad break.*

In Isaiah 43, God says, "When you go through the fire, you will not be burned; the flames will not harm you." It doesn't say *if* you go through the fire; it says *when* you go through. We all go through things that are unfair, things we don't understand. In the fire you have to remind yourself, "This fire is not going to burn me. This challenge is not going to keep me from my dreams. This sickness is not going to stop my purpose. These people who have done me wrong are not going to sour my life." When people met those Hebrew men in years to come, many of them never knew they had been thrown into a fire as teenagers. They never knew they had gone through this huge trial. There was no permanent damage, no scars or bruises. They just saw three healthy and whole men. You may be in the fire now, but as with them, it's not going to set you back permanently. When you come out, you're not going to be scarred for life. There's not going to be any sign of the fire, any sign of the sickness, any sign of the addiction. You're going to come out without the smell of smoke.

In Chapter Two, I mentioned that my mother went through terminal cancer in 1981. When I came home from college for Christmas that year and saw her, I was shocked. She was very sick and frail. She looked as though she was close to death. There was no treatment that doctors could give her. For three years she fought the good fight of faith. It was a struggle, with many difficult, lonely nights. Thoughts told her that she was going to die and that there was a pink dress in her closet that she should be buried in. She was in the fire. The flames were all around her. It didn't look good. But as with the three teenagers, God kept the fire from burning her. When you see my mother today, healthy, strong, and beautiful, she doesn't look as though she's been through terminal cancer. She doesn't look as though she spent three years fighting the fight of her life. She doesn't even look as though she had to raise my brother, Paul.

> *You need to get this down in your spirit:* That fire is not going to burn you.

You may be in the fire now, dealing with a sickness, a financial difficulty, or a child who's off course. You need to get this down in your spirit: *That fire is not going to burn you.* What's come against you is not permanent. Don't believe the lies that it's all downhill from here, that this will always taint your future, that this will always hinder your dreams. What was meant for harm, God is turning to your advantage. When people see you, they're not going to see what you've been through. They're not going to see the mistakes you've made. They're not going to see the disappointments or the people who did you wrong. As with my mother, you're going to be so blessed, so happy, and so healthy that they see who you are and not what you've been through.

No Sign of What You've Been Through

The Israelites were in slavery for 430 years. They were mistreated and taken advantage of. It looked as though that was their destiny. But God supernaturally brought them out of Egypt. As they were leaving, the people who had oppressed them for all those years gave them gold, silver, and clothing. I can imagine the Israelites walking out with those new clothes on, new shoes, wearing jewelry. They didn't look like what they had been through. They didn't leave looking like slaves. They were loaded down with gifts. They traveled through the desert for years, yet the Scripture says, "There was not one sick or feeble one among them." Their clothes and shoes didn't wear out for forty years. They didn't have grocery stores, pharmacies, or hospitals. It was hot and dry, and they lived on the move, yet when people saw them, nobody could tell what they had been through. Nobody could tell they had been slaves and mistreated. Why? When God restores, there is no sign of what you've been through.

You may have been a slave to some things—a slave to addictions, a slave to depression, a slave to fear, poverty, or lack. Perhaps it's been in your family line for generations. You think you're going to look like all those who have gone before you. No, your days of

> *Your days of captivity have come to an end. Freedom is here.*

captivity have come to an end. Freedom is here. God is not going to just deliver you. He's not just going to break bondages. He's going to restore you to where nobody will know you were ever a slave. Nobody will know you were addicted. Nobody will know you were depressed. Nobody will know you came out of dysfunction.

I love the story of our friend Tyler Perry. He grew up poor and mistreated by his father. As a little boy, he had to hide under the porch of their house to escape all the drama and dysfunction in his home. He was in the fire, and it looked as though that fire would stop his destiny. He was just a little boy who had no control of his situation. But the Scripture says that God is a father to the fatherless. When you're in a fire, you can be assured that you're not there by yourself. God shows up in the fiery places. He comes when it's unfair, when you're outnumbered, when it's beyond your control. Tyler has an incredible imagination, and when he was under that front porch, he would make up stories that took him to other places. It gave him a break from the pain and turmoil he was dealing with. It was those stories and his imagination that opened doors to his film and play screenwriting. It opened the door to him becoming one of the most successful entertainers and filmmakers of our day.

When you see Tyler now, so blessed, successful, always smiling, making people laugh, and loving God, he doesn't look like what he's been through. You'd never know he didn't have a great childhood. What happened? God brought him through without the smell of smoke. Nothing that's coming against you is going to keep you from your destiny. Nothing you've been through is going to hinder your future. Don't believe the lies that you've been through too much, that the sickness is too big, that the past was too hurtful, or that you've had too many bad breaks. All that is setting you up for God to show out in your life. Psalm 71 says, "God will restore you to greater honor." The greater the difficulty, the greater the honor. Get this down in your spirit: *You're not going to look like what you've been*

> *Don't believe the lies that you've been through too much, that the sickness is too big, that the past was too hurtful, or that you've had too many bad breaks.*

through. You're going to look like who you are—blessed, prosperous, talented, successful, healthy, whole, victorious.

Restored to Greater Honor

As a teenager, God gave Joseph a dream that one day he would lead a nation. He started off great, being his father's favorite son. Then the bottom dropped out. His brothers were jealous and threw him into a pit to die, then changed their minds and sold him as a slave. He ended up working for an Egyptian army captain, cleaning his house and doing repairs. But someone lied about him, and he was put in prison. Year after year, he sat in a lonely cell,

> *God will not let the actions of other people keep you from your purpose.*

thinking he was forgotten. It looked as though it was permanent. But God will not let the actions of other people keep you from your purpose. If that was the case, they control your destiny and God does not. If something happens that's unfair, you may not like it, but God is going to use it to get you to where you're supposed to be. He wouldn't allow it if He didn't have a purpose.

One day Joseph was called out of the prison to interpret Pharaoh's dream. Pharaoh was so impressed that he made Joseph the prime minister of Egypt. Now Joseph was in charge of the whole country, one of the most powerful people of that day. Joseph wasn't even from Egypt. He didn't have any formal training, he hadn't been raised in the palace, and he wasn't related to Pharaoh. But God knows how to restore you to greater honor. He knows how to make up for what you've been through. I can imagine that when people came to the palace and saw Joseph, they thought he'd been born into royalty, raised in the palace, and educated in the finest schools. They didn't know that years earlier he was sitting in a pit, betrayed by his brothers. They didn't know he was a former slave who'd cleaned houses. They didn't know he'd spent lonely nights sitting in a prison cell. There was no sign of the injustice, no sign of the betrayal, no sign of the lonely nights. All they could see was a man running the country with great influence, prestige, and honor.

That's the way God restores. People won't be able to see what you've been through. As with Joseph, you may be in a situation that's unfair. You're doing the right thing, but the wrong thing is happening. Don't worry. Your time is coming. God is a God of justice. He sees the wrongs. He sees what's unfair, who left you out, who betrayed you. You're going to be restored to greater honor. Because of what tried to stop you, God is going to take you further than if it had not happened. When you get a double dose of trouble, you're going to get a double dose of favor. Now quit believing the lies that you're stuck, that the bad breaks will always limit you, that you'll never get past the divorce, or

> *When you get a double dose of trouble, you're going to get a double dose of favor.*

the financial difficulty, or the sickness. That is not how your story ends. God has the final say. He's says, "I'm going to restore the years that were stolen. I'm going to pay you back for what was unfair." You're not going to come out beat up, bedraggled, hair-singed, clothes burned. You're going to come out without the smell of smoke. Nobody is going to know what you've been through. As with Joseph, all they're going to see is you promoted, honored, and doing great things.

I know a couple who were living a very blessed life, but then the perfect storm hit. Their business went down, the wife had health problems, and one of their in-laws suddenly died. Because of all the hospital bills and extra expenses, they ended up losing their house. They were so discouraged. I told them what I'm telling you: "We all get thrown into the fire at some point, but that fire cannot harm you. God is still on the throne. You stay in faith, and He's going to bring you out better." Sometimes

> *All you have to do is believe. God works where there's an attitude of faith.*

when we hear this, our mind says, *There's no way. How can I get past this? How can I get well?* Joseph could have said, "How can I get out of this prison? I'm a slave and a foreigner. I have no rights." But you don't have to figure it out. All you have to do is believe. God works where there's an attitude of faith. When you're in the fire, instead of complaining, instead of talking about how it's never going to work out, turn it around and say, "Father, thank You that I'm not just coming out, but I'm coming out without the smell of smoke. Thank You that You're going to restore me to greater honor." That's not just being positive, that's releasing your faith.

I saw this same couple several years after that perfect storm hit. The wife showed me a picture of the new house into which they had just moved. She told me how the children had to share a room in their old house, but now they have their own rooms. She told how the new house is closer to her husband's work, and how his new business has taken off. She had big tears streaming down her face and was thanking God for His goodness. When I looked at that new house, and I looked at her, healthy and whole, and I looked at her husband who was beaming with joy, I thought to myself, *You don't look like what you've been through. You came out without the smell of smoke.* That's what God wants to do for you, to restore you to greater honor. Now get a vision for it. Don't go around with a chip on your shoulder, bitter over who did you wrong, discouraged over what didn't work out.

> *Give God something to work with.*

Give God something to work with. "Father, thank You that what was meant for my harm You're turning to my advantage. Thank You that I'm not going to look like what I've been through, but I'm going to look like who You created me to be. I'm going to look blessed, prosperous, strong, healthy, and whole."

He Crosses Lakes

In Mark 5, there was a man who was possessed by evil spirits and lived out in the tombs, which were caves carved out of the rock hills in which the dead were kept. He didn't wear any clothes, his hair was matted, and he couldn't be restrained. They tried chaining his arms and feet in iron shackles, but every time he would break the chains. No one was strong enough to control him. All through the day and night he would wander through the tombs screaming and cutting himself with stones. Everyone knew to stay away from this crazy man. One day Jesus got in a boat, crossed the lake, and went to where this man was. The man came running and fell at His feet. Jesus prayed for him, cast the spirits out, and the man was instantly healed. His mind was restored. Some local people saw it happen, ran and reported it in the town, and the people came out to see. The man had cleaned himself up and put on clothes. The Scripture says, "They saw the man sitting there, fully clothed, in his right mind, perfectly sane." They were amazed and even frightened. They thought, *Wait a minute. We've seen this guy break chains. We know he's deranged. What happened?* It was so far out that they couldn't believe it.

What's interesting is that Jesus made a special trip to cross the lake just to get to this man. After He healed him, Jesus got in the boat and went back. As with this man, sometimes forces of darkness come against us, and we can't get free on our own. The good news is that our God still crosses lakes. When you can't get to Him, He'll come to you. You may have situations that look too far gone, the addiction seems too strong, the sickness is too big, or the family member is too far off course. Nothing is too much for our God. His power is greater than any force that's trying to stop you. He's crossing the lake right now. Those forces that have held you back are being broken. You are not going to live addicted, depressed, sick, or fearful. Chains are being loosed, strongholds are coming down. What you couldn't make happen, the Most High God is making happen.

> *Nothing is too much for our God. His power is greater than any force that's trying to stop you.*

My father had a sister named Mary. When she was in her forties, she became very sick. She couldn't get out of bed, couldn't walk, talk, or feed herself. She got to the point where she didn't recognize people and was going in and out of consciousness. She was at home and had basically been given up to die. When my father heard how bad she was, he drove to where she lived in Dallas to pray for her. He walked in the room, and Mary didn't recognize him. He held her hand and said, "Mary, rise and walk." Immediately, she woke up and got out of bed. She was able to walk and started talking to my father. That day, for the first time in months, she fed herself. It was a turning point. She was completely healed.

Later that night, my father asked her, "Mary, why did you get up so quickly?" She answered, "I heard God say, 'Mary, rise and walk.'" My father laughed and said, "No, Mary. I said that." She replied, "No, John. I heard God say to rise and walk." My father said, "Mary, I was standing right by your bed. I'm the one who said it." She got right up in my father's face and declared, "Listen here, John. I heard the Creator of the universe, the Most High God, say, 'Mary, rise and walk.' When He said it, I felt something go through my body like I've never felt before." What was that? God crossing the lake. God breaking forces of darkness. Mary went on to live many years, healthy and whole. She didn't look like what she had been through.

I can imagine people coming up to the man who had been deranged and asking, "Are you really the same man who was out in the tombs? Are you really that crazy, screaming guy we were all afraid of?" What they were saying was, "You don't look like what you've been through. We saw you one way, but now you're blessed, healthy, free, and doing great things." As he was playing with his grandchildren, enjoying life through the years, he must have paused many times and said, "God, thank You for crossing the lake. Thank You for coming to me when I couldn't come to You." How many times has God crossed the lake for us? How many times has He freed us

> *How many times has God crossed the lake for us?*

when we couldn't free ourselves? How many times has He brought us out of trouble that we got ourselves into, or turned a loved one around who didn't deserve it, or healed us when the medical report said we were done, or promoted us when we didn't have the qualifications. That's the mercy of God. The Scripture says that His mercy is from everlasting to everlasting. That means that God will never stop crossing the lake.

He Brings the Best Robe

In the story of the prodigal son in Luke 15, the young man left home with his father's inheritance and wasted all the money through partying and living wild. He eventually ran out of funds, and the only job he could find was feeding hogs in a field. He got so low, so desperate, that he had to eat the hog food to survive. He finally decided to go back home. He thought, *My father has servants who live better than me. I'll go back and see if he'll hire me as a servant. Maybe I can get a job working with the staff.* When he came home, his father was out looking for him and saw him from a long way off. The father took off running to his son, hugged him and kissed him. The son started in with his speech: "Dad, I know I've done wrong. I know I blew it." His father didn't let him finish. He said to his assistant, "Quick! Bring the best robe in the house and put it on him. Put a ring on his finger and new shoes on his feet. And kill the fatted calf. We're going to have a party."

Now imagine that the son gets cleaned up and is wearing a new robe, new shoes, and the family ring. He doesn't look or smell like the guy from the hog field. He doesn't look like the son who blew his inheritance. This shows us the heart of God. Even when it's our fault, even when we bring the trouble on ourselves, God doesn't want us to look like what we've been through. He doesn't want you to live in the constant memory of the failure, the hurt, or the injustice. Whether you made the mistake or the forces of darkness are trying to stop you as they did the deranged man, God still crosses lakes and He still says to bring the best robe. He still restores us to honor. You would

> *He doesn't look or smell like the guy from the hog field.*

have thought the prodigal's father would say, "Fine, you can come home, but you need to feel sorrier and guiltier and make sure you know how wrong you were." The father didn't even talk to the young man about his mistake.

You may have blown it and done things you're not proud of. You think you'll always be hindered by your past. Quit listening to the accusing voices. You're forgiven. You're redeemed. Now do your part and put on your robe of honor. Receive the mercy that your Heavenly Father is offering you. If you shake off the guilt and keep moving forward, nobody is going to be able to tell what you've been

> *Now do your part and put on your robe of honor.*

through. People will say, "You mean you struggled with an addiction for years? You don't look like it. You're clean, free, and helping others. You don't look like you went through cancer. You're strong and healthy. You don't look like you went through a divorce. You're happy and remarried, with a great spouse." God's dream is to bring you out better.

You may have gone through things that are unfair. It looks as though you're at a disadvantage. No, get ready. God is about to do a new thing. He's crossing the lake. He's coming after you. He's running to you. If you stay in faith, I believe and declare that God is going to restore you to greater honor. Things are changing in your favor right now. Forces of darkness are being broken. Healing, vindication, promotion, and breakthroughs are on the way. You're coming out of that fire without the smell of smoke.

CHAPTER FOURTEEN

A Turnaround Is Coming

When we look at all the difficult situations we face, it's easy to get discouraged, to think they could never change, and accept that they're never going to work out. But God says in Zephaniah 3, "I will turn things around for My people." He's a turnaround God. He turns barren wombs into babies. He turns Red Seas into dry pathways. He turns five loaves and two fish into dinner for thousands. He turns skin filled with leprosy into skin as clear as a baby's. When thoughts tell you, *Your situation is permanent. You'll never get out of this problem, never get well, never see your family restored*, get ready. A turnaround is coming. God is about to turn the sickness into health, turn addictions into freedom, turn the lack into abundance, turn the struggle into ease. You're coming into a turnaround season. You're going to see the hand of God do things that are unusual, uncommon, out of the ordinary.

Mountains into Molehills

This is what God said in the book of Zechariah about the opposition faced by Zerubbabel, the governor of Judah who was in charge of the rebuilding of the temple at Jerusalem: "So, big mountain, who do you think you are? Next to Zerubbabel you're nothing but a molehill." Mountains represent obstacles that look permanent, immovable. Depression can be a mountain with which you feel you'll always have to struggle. A mountain can be people at work who are not for you. They have seniority, so what can you do about it? Or how about a mountain of debt, of lack, of can't get ahead that's been in your family for years. This is a new day. That mountain is about to be turned into a molehill. God is about to flatten some things out. He's about to remove some obstacles. What used to hold you back is not going to limit you anymore. People who weren't for you will suddenly get out of your path. You didn't have to do it. God turned it around. That mountain of loneliness, not having someone in life to love, is about to become a molehill. The right person is going to find you—a divine connection, somebody better than you've imagined.

> *Mountains represent obstacles that look permanent, immovable.*

You have to receive this by faith. This won't do you any good if you think, *This is not for me, Joel. My situation could never turn around. You don't know what I'm facing.* You can cancel out what God wants to do by doubt, by negative thinking. Why don't you be a believer and

> *Whatever you think is permanent, whatever you think you can never get past, you need to see that mountain being turned into a molehill.*

not a doubter? Get in agreement with God and say, "Father, I believe that You promise a turnaround is coming in my health, my finances, my relationships, my career." Whatever you think is permanent, whatever you think you can never get past, you need to see that mountain being turned into a molehill.

In the Scripture, David went through a lot of unjust opposition, betrayals, and lonely nights. King Saul was trying to kill him, and he had a baby son who died. There were plenty of things that could have stopped his destiny. But he says in Psalm 30, "God, You have turned my mourning into dancing. You've turned my sorrow into joy." He could have lived discouraged and bitter, looking in the rearview mirror. But he understood that we serve a turnaround God. Yes, you may have seasons of mourning, times when you go through loss, disappointments, and unfair things. But that's not how your story ends. A turnaround is coming. God is going to take what was meant for your harm and turn it to your advantage. He's not going to stop all the difficulties. He won't keep you from every mountain, but He promises He will turn the sorrow into joy, the mountain into a molehill. Weeping may endure for a night, but joy is coming in the morning. You have to get your fire back. The disappointment, the loss, or what you're up against now doesn't stop your purpose. God is still in control. He didn't bring you this far to leave you. It seems as though it's a setback, but it's really a setup for God to show out in a greater way.

The prophet Zephaniah went on to say that when God turns it around, "Everything you've lost will be restored. Instead of shame, He will give you honor. Burdens you've carried will be lifted. He will get rid of all those who have made your life miserable. He will heal

> *"Everything you've lost will be restored."*

the sick. He will bring home the prodigals. You will be respected wherever you go." You need to get this down in your spirit. It's turnaround time. What's limited you in the past is not going to limit you anymore.

The God of the Turnaround

When I look back over my life, I can see the God of the turnaround. In previous chapters, I described how my mother was diagnosed with terminal cancer in 1981, and there was no treatment the doctors could give her. It was Christmas, and we were expecting to have a joyful time with all the family together, but instead it was a time of weeping. I had never seen my mother sick a day in her life. She was only forty-six years old, but now she was frail, very weak, with yellow skin. As a family, we did what I'm asking you to do. We said, "Father, this looks impossible to us, but we know You're a turnaround God, You can turn this mountain into a molehill." The psalmist says, "The moment you pray, the tide of the battle turns." Something supernatural happens when you pray in faith. The turnaround God goes to work. Miracles are set in motion, angels are dispatched, and favor is released. Don't just think about your problems. Don't just worry about it and live stressed. Go to God in prayer. Ask Him to turn it around. Ask Him to heal you, to free you, to favor you, to bring dreams to pass, to level that mountain. Don't beg Him and say, "Oh, God, please, You have to do it." No, go to Him in faith and say, "Father, I know You're bigger than this cancer. You're stronger than this opposition. You're more powerful than this addiction. I'm asking You to make a way where I don't see a way."

> *Something supernatural happens when you pray in faith.*

Here's the key: Once you pray, believe that it's already done. You may not see it with your physical eyes. Most of the time it doesn't happen instantly. There's usually a period from when you pray to when the answer shows up. That's a test of your faith. Thoughts will say, *Nothing happened. It's not going to work out. This turnaround thing is not for you.* Don't believe those lies. In the unseen realm, the turnaround is already in motion. What God promised is already en route. Instead of going downhill as the medical report said about my mother, she started getting better, slowly defying the odds. Her skin went back to its normal color. She got her energy back and gained her weight back. Over forty years later, she's still healthy and whole. What was that? The turnaround God. We can say with David, "God has turned our sorrow into joy. He's turned our mourning into dancing."

> *Once you pray, believe that it's already done.*

You may have situations that look permanent. All the circumstances say, "It will never work out. It's been too long. The odds are against you." God is not limited by what limits us. We're natural; He's supernatural. He's saying to you today, "A turnaround is coming." He's going to turn sickness into health as He did for my mother. He's going to turn loneliness into companionship. He's going to turn the child who's off course back into his purpose. He's going to turn the people who are against you to be for you. He's going to turn the dream that looks too far gone into a reality. This is a turnaround day. You're going to see mountains turned into molehills. What was meant to stop you is going to be turned to push you into your destiny.

> *God is not limited by what limits us.*

Turning Hearts in Your Favor

When we were trying to acquire the Compaq Center, we needed ten votes from the city council members. We worked for a year and a half and finally convinced ten council members, exactly what we needed. But two days before the main vote, one of the council members who was for us received so much pressure from the other side that he decided to be out of town for the vote. His absence was like a no vote. We wouldn't get the facility. We couldn't believe it. It was the last moment. We had worked all this time, and now we were one vote shy. So I went to talk with a young Jewish council member who had been against us the whole time. I thought I had nothing to lose. When I walked into his office, he said, "Joel, I've changed my mind. I'm going to vote for you." I nearly passed out. He told me he had gotten a phone call the day before from an older Jewish woman he knew when he was growing up. He always had great respect for her. He hadn't spoken with her in over twenty years, but she had called and told him in no uncertain terms that he was to vote for Lakewood to get the Compaq Center. He changed his mind, and his vote gave us the facility.

God knows how to turn people who are against you and cause them to be for you. I had tried to convince him with everything I had, giving him my best speeches. What I couldn't do in over a year to change his mind, God did in a five-minute phone call from a woman I had never met. When God is ready to turn it around, no person can stop Him. No sickness, no addiction, and no trouble can stop Him. What God has purposed for your life will come to pass. He will do it when you face these situations that seem permanent, when you've done all you can and the door hasn't opened, when the person hasn't changed, when the medical report hasn't improved. You feel as we did, that it's too late and you've run out of options. No, get ready. A turnaround is coming. What God started, He's going to finish. There's not a mountain you face that He can't turn into a molehill. He can change the mind of any person who is against you. You don't have to convince people. You do your part and leave the rest to God. When the supervisor isn't treating you right, keep doing the right thing and let God deal with

> *What I couldn't do in over a year to change his mind, God did in a five-minute phone call from a woman I had never met.*

them. The Scripture says, "God can turn the heart of a king." God knows how to turn people to be for you. He can cause them to want to be good to you.

A friend of mine who is from Europe and works here in the United States had a problem with his visa. He went to the government office to get it extended, but the man at the counter was very rude and unhelpful, acting as though my friend was bothering him. The man took his paperwork, barely even looked at it, and said, "It will be five years before this is approved." My friend pleaded with him, asking if there was anything he could do to make it happen faster. The man got more upset, said they were all backed up, that this was the policy, and there was nothing more he could do about it. My friend left the office very discouraged. There were no good options. He couldn't operate his business without the paperwork. Two weeks later, he got a call from that government office saying that his paperwork had been approved and was ready to be picked up. He rushed down there, believing for the best, but in the back of his mind he was thinking it was a mistake. When he walked into the office, the man who had been so rude was holding the paperwork. My friend thanked him and said, "Wow, this is such a great surprise! I thought it was going to take much longer." The man replied gruffly, "It should have, but ever since I met you,

I can't get you off my mind. I wake up thinking about you. I eat breakfast thinking about you. I come to work thinking about you. Just take the paperwork and go so I can have some peace." God knows how to turn people around. They may not like you, but they will help you fulfill your purpose.

> *They may not like you, but they will help you fulfill your purpose.*

Great Sorrow into Great Joy

In Luke 7, Jesus had left Capernaum and was headed to the city of Nain. His disciples and a large group of people were following Him. When He arrived at the city, a funeral procession was coming toward Him. They were on their way to bury a young boy whose mother was a widow. She had already buried her husband, and now she was about to bury her only son. You can imagine the sorrow and pain she was dealing with. In those days, her son represented her security, how she would be taken care of in her later years. The Scripture says, "When Jesus saw her, His heart broke." God sees when you're hurting. He sees when you're lonely, when you feel so overwhelmed that you don't think you can go on. He is moved with compassion. Jesus went over to the woman and said, "Don't cry." He was saying, "You're weeping now, but I'm about to turn things around. This pain is not permanent. This sorrow is not how your story ends."

Jesus walked over to the coffin, and the pallbearers set it down. They didn't know what was happening. Jesus spoke to the boy and said, "Young man, wake up." The son who had been dead sat up in the coffin and began to look around. Jesus went over, picked him up, and handed him to his mother alive and well. She went from great sorrow to great joy, from great mourning to great rejoicing. This mother had been depressed, distraught, not know-ing how she could go on, but the God of the turnaround stepped in. Now she was still weeping, but these were no longer tears of sadness, they were tears of joy. Sometimes life gets tough. You shed tears from hurts, from a bad medical report, from a child who breaks your heart, from

> *This mother had been depressed, distraught, not knowing how she could go on, but the God of the turnaround stepped in.*

dreams that don't work out. There will be times of mourning, but I want you to see that it is not the end. We serve a turnaround God. As with this woman, He's going to step in and turn the sor-row into joy, turn the brokenness into wholeness, turn the mourn-ing into dancing.

Imagine this solemn funeral procession on their way to the burial grounds, with all the weeping and mourning, and people stepping out of the way respectfully. Then Jesus meets the woman and raises the little boy. They don't continue on to the cemetery. They don't keep going to the burial plot. They turn around and go back into the city. People start asking, "Why are you back so soon? Why didn't you bury him?" They answer, "There's no need. We had a turnaround, something unexpectedly changed in our favor."

We all have situations at times that look dead, dreams that we've given up on, and promises that seem as though it's too late. God is saying, "I'm going to bring dead things back to life." There are going to be turnarounds that leave you in awe. You left defeated, but you're going to come back victorious. You thought your busi-ness was dead, but God is about to surprise you. Increase is com-ing, favor is coming, and new clients are coming. You thought you'd have to live with the sickness or just manage the depression. No, a turnaround is coming. God is about to do something out

> *There are going to be turnarounds that leave you in awe.*

of the ordinary, something supernatural. As with these people, you're going to be in awe, amazed at the greatness of God.

Something Unexpected, Something Awesome

I met a man who had been very healthy, had a great family and successful career, but in his mid-fifties he had what appeared to be a massive stroke and was left brain dead. His family was so distraught. The neurosurgeon was a close friend of the family and a leading expert. He said, "Unfortunately, there's nothing we can do." There was no brain activity. The man was on a breathing machine that was keeping him alive. The family made arrangements to have his organs donated and said their good-byes. They were told that once they took out the breathing tube, he would stop breathing on his own in a couple of minutes. They removed the life support, the family waited for him to pass, but he kept breathing on his own. The doctor said that wasn't completely uncommon, and it was just a matter of time. The family went home and started making plans for the funeral. A few hours later, a nurse called and said frantically, "You have to get up here! He woke up! He's talking, and he wants something to eat." The doctors had no explanation. Today, this man is totally well.

God has the final say. Yes, at some point we're all going to pass, but it's not over until God says it's over. This man's family went from making plans for a funeral to making plans for dinner that night. From great sorrow to great joy. We serve a turnaround God. You may have gone through disappointments, a rough childhood, an illness that set you back. You may feel that heaviness, have lost your passion, and think this is all you have to look forward to. No, there's a turnaround coming. Something unexpected is going to change in your favor.

> *This man's family went from making plans for a funeral to making plans for dinner that night.*

In previous chapters, I mentioned the story in the Scripture of the young lady named Ruth whose husband passed away. She never dreamed she would be a widow at such a young age. You can imagine the heartache and sadness. When her mother-in-law, Naomi, who was a widow as well, decided to move back to Bethlehem, Ruth went along to help take care of her. They had no income, and they were both heartbroken. To survive, every morning Ruth went into the harvest fields to pick up wheat that the workers had missed. It looked as though lack, struggle, and loneliness were all Ruth had to look forward to. But the owner of the field told his workers to leave handfuls of wheat on purpose for Ruth, and suddenly Ruth had more than enough. God took care of Ruth.

If the story stopped there, it would be a great story. But when God turns things around, He pays you back for what wasn't fair. He brings you out better. The owner of that field fell in love with Ruth, and they ended up getting married. Now she didn't have to work in the fields; she owned the fields. God turned the lack into abundance, turned her loneliness into a marriage with a successful, godly man. They had a baby named Obed, who had a son named Jesse, who had a son named David. Ruth became the great grandmother of the greatest king who ever lived. God knows how to turn sorrow into joy and mourning into dancing. You may have been through loss, things that weren't fair. You could easily live discouraged, thinking you've seen your best days. If you only knew what God was up to. He has turnarounds in your future that are so

> *Now she didn't have to work in the fields; she owned the fields.*

awesome that you won't think about what you've lost. You'll be so blessed, so happy, and so fulfilled that you don't look back. You'll move forward in faith, filled with gratitude, thanking God for what He's done.

From the Back to the Front

I talked with a single mom who was struggling to make ends meet, working two jobs and long hours. She felt badly that she couldn't be with her children more. On top of that, she had no time for herself, no time to date or have a social life. It looked as though that's the way it would always be. She couldn't see anything changing. But just because you don't see it doesn't mean that God is not up to something. You don't know who He's speaking to about you, what He's lining up to come your way. You keep being faithful and you're going to come into handfuls on purpose as Ruth did. You'll come into blessings, healing, and relationships that you didn't see coming.

One day her neighbors invited this young lady and her children for dinner. She had only met this couple one time. At dinner that night, the couple told her that they thought she was a great mother and such a hard worker. They said, "We want to do something to make your life a little easier," then they handed her the keys to a brand-new car. She couldn't believe it. She didn't see that coming and was so grateful. She was able to sell her old car, pay off her debts, and cut back on her hours at work. About a year later, she met an executive from a large company and they fell in love. Today, she's happily married and her children are flourish-ing. She told me, "I never dreamed I could be this blessed, this fulfilled." That's the God of a turn-around. You may be in a season of struggle, a season of hardship when you're working long hours, doing your best to provide, but nothing is improving. You don't see how it can ever change. God is watching you. He sees your sacrifice. He sees you going the extra mile. You're going to come into these turnaround moments when God is going to turn the struggle into ease, turn the lack into abundance, turn the sorrow into joy, turn the injustice into vindication. He going to turn what you didn't get and what wasn't fair into fulfillment, into purpose, into a blessed, satisfied life.

> *You're going to come into these turnaround moments when God is going to turn the struggle into ease, turn the lack into abundance, turn the sorrow into joy, turn the injustice into vindication.*

I was in line with my children for a popular ride at an amuse-ment park years ago. It was single file at first, but when we got close to the front, we had to go into a room that was about twenty feet by twenty feet and wait. We were the first ones in the room and walked to the two big doors at the front, but other people came in and started maneuvering their way in front of us, mostly kids. I didn't feel like trying to hold our ground at the front, so we eventu-ally ended up at the very back of the room. A lady came out, stood at the front where everyone had crowded, and gave us instructions about the ride. We were standing near the back doors where we'd come into the room. She said, "Okay, we're ready to go. Everyone turn around and go back out the same doors you came in." All of a sudden we were at the front instead of the back of the line.

You may feel as though you're falling behind, that everyone

is getting ahead of you. You've had some bad breaks, and people are manipulating things. Don't worry. A turnaround is coming. God knows how to take you from the back to the front, from being overlooked to standing out, from working in the fields to owning the fields. You are coming into a turnaround season. The turnaround God is about to make happen what you couldn't make happen. Even now, He's turning sickness into health, turning borrowing into lending, turning sorrows into joy, turning addictions into freedom. What's hindered you in the past is not permanent. The trouble at work is about to turn around. The child who is off course is about to turn around. The depression you've been dealing with is about to turn around. This is a new day. Forces that have held you back are being broken. I believe and declare what Zephaniah prophesied, that everything you've lost will be restored. Instead of shame, you will have honor. Burdens you've carried are being lifted. People who have hindered you are being moved out of the way. The sick are being healed, the prodigals are coming home, and you will be respected everywhere you go. It's turnaround time.

CHAPTER FIFTEEN

The Best Is Next

It's easy to get satisfied with where we are. When we've seen blessing and favor, when God has protected us, promoted us, and opened doors, we can start thinking that we've seen our best days. But God never does His greatest feats in your yesterdays; they are always in your future. The Scripture says, "The path of the righteous gets brighter and brighter." What God has in front of you is more fulfilling and more rewarding than anything you've seen in the past. But sometimes before it gets brighter, it gets darker. Before we see more than enough, we go through a season of not enough. There are times when the good has to come to an end in order to make room for the best. But it doesn't make sense to us. "Why did my business slow down? Why did this person walk away? Why did this door close?" It's all a part of God's plan. He's shaking things up to move you out of the good and into the best. If He didn't close those doors, you wouldn't see the fullness of your destiny.

We may not like the process. It's uncomfortable. We're doing the right thing but the wrong thing is happening. We're working hard but not seeing increase. Thoughts will tell you, *It's never going to get better.* Don't believe the lies. The disappointment, the breakup, and the slow season didn't stop what God has for you. It's getting you in position for favor that you've never seen. You had a relationship that didn't work out, but God knew it was going to happen. That didn't catch Him off guard. He's already lined up someone better than you can imagine.

> *That setback is not stopping you; it's setting you up for new levels.*

Perhaps your business has slowed down or a contract didn't work out. That setback is not stopping you; it's setting you up for new levels. You're going to come out, not as you were before, but healthier, stronger, promoted, and increased.

When You're Running Out

In John 2, Jesus was at a wedding in Galilee. It was a big celebration with hundreds of people. Everything was going great until they ran out of wine. Jesus' mother came and told him about the problem. Jesus had not performed any miracles in public up to this point, but she knew something about Jesus that others didn't know. She told the work staff to do whatever He told them to do. There were six large water pots over to the side. Each pot held from twenty to thirty gallons. Jesus told the men to fill them with water. I can imagine them thinking, *What good is that going to do?* Instead of talking themselves out of it, they filled the containers to the brim. Then Jesus

> *If the wine had not run out, if they had not come to the end of what they were used to, they would never have seen the best wine. God saves the best for next.*

said, "Now dip some out and take it to the master of ceremonies, to the man who's in charge of the banquet." The Scripture says, "When the master of ceremonies tasted the water that was now wine, he called the groom over and said, 'Usually a host serves the best wine first. Then, when everyone is full and doesn't know any better, he brings out the less expensive wine. But you have saved the best until now!" Notice how God works: If the wine had not run out, if they had not come to the end of what they were used to, they would never have seen the best wine. God saves the best for next.

You may feel as though you're coming to an end. You're running out of opportunities, and the doors are closing. You're running out of favor, and what used to work is not working. You're running out of resources and having a hard time making ends meet. Maybe you're running out of strength. You're weary and feel that you can't take it anymore. This may seem odd, but you're in a good place. When you come to the end, that's when God steps in and not only helps you get through it, but He says, "I've saved the best for next." He's saved the best position, the best relationships, and the best in your finances—you have more than you've ever had. He has the best in your health—you feel better than you've ever felt. He has the best in your family—you're happier than you've ever been. The fact that things are running out doesn't mean that God has forgotten about you, or that you must have run out of favor, or that you must have done something wrong. It's a sign that God is about to do something that you've never seen.

One translation says that Jesus' mother said to Him, "They have no more wine." Sometimes we feel like we have "no more"— no more strength, no more vision, no more health. That's okay. There are seasons when you come to an end, when you run out of a good thing. The first wine that the people had at the banquet was fine. Nobody complained, they were blessed, having a great celebration, but the wine was supposed to run out. It was a part of God's plan. If it hadn't run out, they would never have seen the best wine. What runs out in your life is not a surprise to God. The relationship that didn't make it, the company that let you go, the loved one you lost, or the health that went down is not a surprise to Him. That doesn't mean you've seen your best days and now you should just sit back and endure it. It means that new levels of favor are coming, new levels of your destiny—better health, better opportunities, better relationships. God doesn't bring you out the same.

> *What runs out in your life is not a surprise to God.*

You're going to look back and say, as that master of ceremonies said, "You've saved the best for now." Don't get bitter about the person who walked away. They had to go so the best could show up. When you see what God does, who He brings, you'll say, "I'm glad that old wine ran out. I'm glad the old boyfriend left. Look what the Lord has done." When the coworkers played politics, made you look bad, and kept you from the promotion, you thought you ran out of favor, that God had forgotten about you. No, that had to happen. When you see the new door God opens and how He promotes you in the presence of your enemies, how He gives you influence and favor that you've never seen, you'll say, "Lord, thank You for saving the best for now. You took me where I couldn't go on my own."

Don't be discouraged when something doesn't work out, something runs out, and you feel as though you're at the end. You've studied your situation, and you've tried to come up with a solution, but you've run out of options. You don't see how your business can make it, or how your marriage will last, or how your health will turn around. When you come to the end, it's a good place. When you can't figure out a solution, that's when God steps in. You had to run out of wine before you could see the best wine. You had to come to an end so God can take you to a new level, so He can open doors bigger than you've imagined, so He can give you health, strength, peace, and joy like you've never seen. The best is not behind you; the best is next.

> *When you come to the end, it's a good place. When you can't figure out a solution, that's when God steps in.*

Now, it may look just the opposite. When you're running low, when you've come to an end, thoughts will tell you, *It's all downhill from here. You're running out of time, and you can't accomplish your dream. You're running out of favor, and business is slowing down. You're running out of strength, and this illness is going to sink you.* The only reason you're running out is because God saved the best for next. Keep the right perspective and say, "Father, this looks like the end, but I know it's a sign that You're about to show out in my life."

When You're at the End of Your Rope

Weddings during Jesus' time would go on for several days. When He showed up, they could have been there enjoying the first wine for days. They were happy, the first wine was good, and no one was complaining. When life is good for us, when we're happy, when our children are blessed and we're seeing favor, we have no complaints, but sometimes things change. We're facing an illness, a child gets off course, or a friend we were counting on walks away. It's easy to live discouraged, to feel as though we're going backward, running out of favor, or running out of health, but there's only one reason you're running out—the good is about to give way to the best. God loves you too much to leave you just with the good wine. That's fine for a season, but at some point you'll come to the end so He can show out in your life in a much greater way.

It's significant that God could have given them the same wine. That would have been a great miracle. We would be telling that story, that God can restore, that when you run out, He can give you more. That's good, but God is so loving, so merciful, that He doesn't bring you out the same. He gives you the best wine. The best is simply something that you've never seen. It's favor that you've never seen, health that you've never seen, opportunity, finances, influence. The best is in front of you. After you see that best, God will give you something better, a new best. That's what it means when He says He's taking you from glory to glory. In between those glories, there will be seasons when you feel as though you have no more. You have nothing more to give, no more creativity, no more resources, no more options. There's nothing wrong with saying, "God, I have no more. I've run out of wine."

> *The best is in front of you. After you see that best, God will give you something better, a new best.*

I mentioned previously that Jesus says, "You are blessed when you're at the end of your rope. With less of you there is more of God and His favor." That seems odd. We're blessed when we're at the end. Why would Jesus say, "We're blessed when the contract doesn't go through. We're blessed when that person walks away"? It's because when you're at the end, when you've run out of options, when you don't have any more wine, that's when God shows up and gives you the best wine. That's when He does more than you can imagine.

Stay on the High Road

A friend of mine played professional football fo[r] was a great player, very popular and well liked. When he retired, he was hired by his team to help develop the players and keep them motivated. For years he was very successful. The team, the coaches, and the players all loved him. You couldn't find a more talented, kind, or loyal person. Life was good. He was seeing favor, increase, and blessing. But one day the owner of the team hired a new manager who didn't like my friend. This manager saw how popular my friend was, and he started poisoning the staff, spreading things that weren't true. Eventually he fired my friend. It was very unfair, very hurtful. When I called to encourage him, he was disappointed but he wasn't discouraged. He understood this principle: When the old wine runs out, that means the best wine is coming, something that you've never seen.

That's why you shouldn't fight every closed door, people who do you wrong, seasons of slow down, or times when you're not seeing the favor you once did. These things have to happen for you to see the best wine, for you to see greater favor and greater influence. As much as we don't like the bad breaks, the betrayals, the disappointments, and the times when people do us wrong, they are all a part of God's plan. God is not only ordering your steps; He's ordering the steps of those you need to help fulfill your destiny. We know that God ordered Jesus' steps, but He also used Judas's betrayal of Jesus as the means to bring Him to be condemned and crucified for our salvation. God ordered Goliath's steps to come against David as the means to David's stepping to the throne. God used my father's going to be with the Lord, something that I didn't like, as the means to get me to step up to pastor the church. When things run out in your life, instead of complaining and being bitter, keep the right perspective. It had to run out so you can see the best wine, so you can step up to who you were created to be.

My friend stayed on the high road. The whole time his supervisor was trying to make him look bad, to engage him in conflict, he wouldn't take the bait. The manager moved someone into his office without asking him, but my friend didn't say a word. He left résumés on my friend's desk for his same position, trying to intimidate him, but my friend ignored it. When he was fired, he wouldn't talk to the press. He didn't make the man look bad. He let God fight his battles. He knew God was his vindicator. He sent me a list of declarations he made every day: "No weapon formed against me will prosper. I will look in triumph on those who have hated me. What was meant for my harm, God is turning to my advantage." What you're doing in the running-out seasons is very important. If you go around bitter, discouraged, and trying to get even, that's going to keep you where you are.

About six months after my friend was fired, he received a phone call from the headquarters of the NFL and was offered the same position he had been doing for his former team, but this time it was for multiple teams over a whole region. Now the NFL, the biggest sports league in the world, is behind him. He has incredible influence and favor. This would never have happened if the old wine had not run out. When doors close, when things slow down, when people turn on you, stay in peace. God knows what He's doing. You're coming to an end, not because it's over, but because the best is next. You're going to see favor that you haven't seen, opportunity

> You're coming to an end, not because it's over, but because the best is next.

that you didn't expect, increase, strength, creativity, good health, more than you've imagined.

When the wine ran out at the wedding, Jesus told the staff

to fill the pots with water. That seemed odd. They needed wine, not water. Sometimes God will ask you to do things you don't understand. He has the best wine ready. He has something that you haven't seen, but it's dependent on your obedience. Will you do what He's asking you to do? It may be to forgive someone who did you wrong. That doesn't seem to make sense. That person hurt you, and you feel you have a right to be bitter. But that will keep you from the best wine. Or God may ask you to step out in faith when you don't feel qualified for a promotion, to teach a class, to start a business, or to mentor a young person. Or it may be to keep a good attitude when you're not being treated right. It's to stay on the high road as my friend did and let God fight your battles. It's easy to try to pay people back, to make them look bad, to do to them what they're doing to you. Trust God to be your vindicator. He can vindicate you better than you can vindicate yourself.

My friend's manager was so against him and so dishonest that eventually he was fired by the team's ownership in a very public way. Everything he had been doing—the schemes, the backbiting, the jealousy—all came to light. Now he's out, and my friend is in, and in a much better position. People can't stop your destiny. Closed doors can't stop your purpose. Bad breaks can't keep you from what God has ordained. When the wine runs out, keep doing what God asks

> *When the wine runs out, keep doing what God asks you to do.*

you to do. Keep being good to people, keep giving, serving, and expecting. The wine that's running out is a sign that the best wine is coming.

From Running Out to Running Over

There was a widow in the Old Testament whose husband had died. Now she was living alone with her son. They got along fine for a while, but then a drought came. Their crops dried up, and their income went down. She used the funds her husband had left, and now those funds had run out. It was a perfect storm. She had no income, no savings, and finally no food. Everything came to an end, and she was preparing their last meal. She and her son were going to eat it, and they had already accepted the fact that this would be it. When the prophet Elijah saw her picking up sticks to make a fire, he said, "Do me a favor. I'm hungry, so will you make me something to eat?" I'm sure she thought, *You have to be kidding.* She said, "Elijah, I promise you that all I have is a little flour and a little oil. We've exhausted all our resources, and I only have enough for me and my son. Once I cook this, we're done."

Elijah asked her to do something that seemed selfish. He said, "Go ahead and make that last meal, but first make me a little loaf of bread." She could have immediately thought, *We're about to starve to death and you want me to feed you before I feed myself and my son? I'm not going to do that.* But then Elijah continued, "For this is what the Lord, the God of Israel, says, 'There will always be plenty of flour and plenty of oil in your cabinets until the time the Lord sends rain and the crops begin to produce again.'" This widow took a step of faith and did as Elijah told her, and from that day forward, week after week, month after month, for three and a half years, the oil never ran out and the flour container was never empty. She had supernatural provision. She went from running out to running over. The running out is a sign that running over is coming. You may feel as though you're running out of strength today, that you're weary from everything that's going on. Get ready, for running over strength is coming. It's a strength that you've never felt, energy like you've never seen. Perhaps you're running out of resources, and your business has slowed down. Get ready, for running over resources are headed your way. If you're running out of favor, not getting any good breaks, and stuck in your career, because you honor God, running over favor is coming,

> *For three and a half years, the oil never ran out and the flour container was never empty. She had supernatural provision.*

running over blessing, running over opportunities. That means you will have so many opportunities that you can't take them all. You'll have to choose which ones you want.

Elijah said, "Make me a loaf of bread first." God is saying, "Keep Me first place in your life." When you wake up in the morning, don't meet with anyone until you first meet with God. Take time to thank Him for the day, to thank Him for who He is, to thank Him that He is the giver of all good things. Thank Him that He's your protector, your provider, your healer, your way maker. All through the day, under your breath, you can talk to God and say, "Lord, thank You for watching over my children. Lord, help me to be my best at work today. Lord, thank You for giving me wisdom." The Scripture says, "If you acknowledge God in all your ways, He'll crown your efforts with success."

Every time God asks you to do a hard thing, that means there's a big blessing coming. It was a sacrifice for the widow to first make Elijah a meal. It took trust, courage, and faith. It wasn't easy for the workers

> *Every time God asks you to do a hard thing, that means there's a big blessing coming.*

to fill the water pots with water. Thoughts were telling them, *You're wasting your time.* They had to fight off the doubts, fight off negative thoughts. But when you choose to obey, when you do the right thing when it's hard, you're setting yourself up for God to show out in your life, to see supernatural favor, supernatural healing, supernatural provision.

The Best Part Is the Next Part

In Chapter Six, I described how a few years after I started pastoring, the church began to grow and we needed a larger auditorium. My father had said over and over that he would never move Lakewood. I was new, and I wasn't about to rock the boat. So I started looking for land around our old location. We found a hundred acres that was right off the freeway and about two miles from where we were. It seemed perfect. A few months later, we went to sign all the papers and close on the property, but the secretary walked out and said, "I'm sorry, but the owner sold this property last night." I couldn't believe it. He didn't keep his word. I was so discouraged. When I went home and told Victoria, she started preaching one of my own messages to me. "Joel, this closed door means God has something better. We're going to stay in faith." I didn't want to hear that. I wanted that property. Then a couple months later, we found another hundred acres that seemed like an even better location, with better access from the freeway. I knew that's why God shut the other door. We went to close on the property, and the same thing happened. They sold it to someone else. We were running out of options. There weren't any more large tracts of land off the freeway in that area. Sometimes God won't step in until you run out of options. The old wine has to run out.

I was tempted to live stressed and worried, but I could hear that still small voice saying, "Joel, trust Me. I'm still in control." I didn't see how it could happen, but God has ways we've never thought of. His plan for your life is better than your own. Many times what we think is the best is far less than what God has in mind. I was hoping to find land to build an auditorium. I never dreamed that God would give

> *You haven't seen, heard, or imagined what God has in store.*

us an already built auditorium on the busiest freeway, the most visible, the most attended, and one of the most prestigious facilities in our city—the former Compaq Center. I had been complaining about running out of options, and all the while God had something better than I ever dreamed. Can I tell you that you haven't seen your best days? You may feel stuck, doors have closed, and the wine has run out. That all happened for a reason. It had to run out so you could see the best wine. The best part of your life is not behind you; the best part of your life is the next part of your life. You haven't seen, heard, or imagined what God has in store. You wouldn't be discouraged about the door that closed if you knew what God was about to open. You wouldn't be stressed about the deal that fell through if you knew your Compaq Center was up ahead. You would put God first place and obey, you would first make the prophet a meal, if you knew supernatural provision is coming.

Sometimes we think that we're running out of time. *It's too late to accomplish my dream. I missed my chance, Joel. I made too many mistakes. I'm too old.* In the Scripture, that's probably the way Caleb felt. He was one of the two Israelite spies who came back from the

Promised Land and told Moses that they were well able to take the land, that they should go in at once. But the negative report from the other ten spies caused the entire Israelite nation to get discouraged, so they turned around and went back into the desert. Caleb was forty years old at the time. For forty years he wandered with them in the desert.

> *Don't settle for a watered-down version of your dream.*

The interesting thing is that it wasn't his fault. He had faith, he was courageous, and he was obedient. It looked as though the other spies had stopped his dream, that their negative report kept him from his destiny. The good news is that what God starts, He's going to finish. What He promised, He's going to bring to pass. When Caleb was eighty-five years old, God said to him, "I haven't forgotten about you. I said you'd go into the Promised Land, and you're still going to go in."

There were three giants living on the land that Caleb wanted. He could have said, "God, give me another place. Those people are too big. I'm too old to fight them." No, don't settle for a watered-down version of your dream. At eighty-five, Caleb said, "God, I still want that mountain." He went into the Promised Land and defeated those giants. It's not too late for you to become all you were created to be. God has not forgotten about the dreams He put in your heart. You're not running out of time; you're running into time.

> *Get ready. The best is next.*

God is ordering your steps. You may think you missed opportunities that didn't happen years earlier, but it wasn't the right time. The door had to close, the people had to be against you, and the business had to not make it. It was all setting you up for the best wine. God saves the best for next. I believe and declare that you're about to come into some bests—best opportunities, best relationships, best health, best resources. As that widow did, because you keep God first place, you're going to go from running out to running over, from not enough to more than enough. Your latter days will be better than your former days. Get ready. The best is next.

ACKNOWLEDGMENTS

In this book I offer many stories shared with me by friends, members of our congregation, and people I've met around the world. I appreciate and acknowledge their contributions and support. Some of those mentioned in the book are people I have not met personally, and in a few cases, we've changed the names to protect the privacy of individuals. I give honor to all those to whom honor is due. As the son of a church leader and a pastor myself, I've listened to countless sermons and presentations, so in some cases I can't remember the exact source of a story.

I am indebted to the amazing staff of Lakewood Church, the wonderful members of Lakewood who share their stories with me, and those around the world who generously support our ministry and make it possible to bring hope to a world in need. I am grateful to all those who follow our services on television, the Internet, SiriusXM, and through the podcasts. You are all part of our Lakewood family.

I offer special thanks also to all the pastors across the country who are members of our Champions Network.

Once again, I am grateful for a wonderful team of professionals who helped me put this book together for you. Leading them is my FaithWords/Hachette publisher, Daisy Hutton, along with team members Patsy Jones and Dale Wilsterman. I truly appreciate the editorial contributions of wordsmith Lance Wubbels.

I am grateful also to my literary agents Jan Miller Rich and Shannon Marven at Dupree Miller & Associates.

And last but not least, thanks to my wife, Victoria, and our children, Jonathan and Alexandra, who are my sources of daily inspiration, as well as our closest family members, who serve as day-to-day leaders of our ministry, including my mother, Dodie; my brother, Paul, and his wife, Jennifer; my sister Lisa and her husband, Kevin; and my brother-in-law Don and his wife, Jackelyn.

We Want to Hear from You!

Each week, I close our international television broadcast by giving the audience an opportunity to make Jesus the Lord of their lives. I'd like to extend that same opportunity to you. Are you at peace with God? A void exists in every person's heart that only God can fill. I'm not talking about joining a church or finding religion. I'm talking about finding life and peace and happiness. Would you pray with me today? Just say, "Lord Jesus, I repent of my sins. I ask You to come into my heart. I make You my Lord and Savior."

Friend, if you prayed that simple prayer, I believe you have been "born again." I encourage you to attend a good Bible-based church and keep God in first place in your life. For free information on how you can grow stronger in your spiritual life, please feel free to contact us.

Victoria and I love you, and we'll be praying for you. We're believing for God's best for you, that you will see your dreams come to pass. We'd love to hear from you!

To contact us, write to:

Joel and Victoria Osteen
PO Box #4271
Houston, TX 77210

Or you can reach us online at www.joelosteen.com.